The Power of Global Teams

By the same author:
Breaking Through Culture Shock: What You Need to Succeed in International Business

The Power of Global Teams

Driving Growth and Innovation in a Fast Changing World

Elisabeth Marx

© Elisabeth Marx 2013

Softcover reprint of the hardcover 1st edition 2013 978-1-137-00811-4

All rights reserved. No reproduction, copy or transmission of this publication may be made without written permission.

No portion of this publication may be reproduced, copied or transmitted save with written permission or in accordance with the provisions of the Copyright, Designs and Patents Act 1988, or under the terms of any licence permitting limited copying issued by the Copyright Licensing Agency, Saffron House, 6–10 Kirby Street, London EC1N 8TS.

Any person who does any unauthorized act in relation to this publication may be liable to criminal prosecution and civil claims for damages.

The author has asserted her right to be identified as the author of this work in accordance with the Copyright, Designs and Patents Act 1988.

First published 2013 by
PALGRAVE MACMILLAN

Palgrave Macmillan in the UK is an imprint of Macmillan Publishers Limited, registered in England, company number 785998, of Houndmills, Basingstoke, Hampshire RG21 6XS.

Palgrave Macmillan in the US is a division of St Martin's Press LLC, 175 Fifth Avenue, New York, NY 10010.

Palgrave Macmillan is the global academic imprint of the above companies and has companies and representatives throughout the world.

Palgrave® and Macmillan® are registered trademarks in the United States, the United Kingdom, Europe and other countries.

ISBN 978-1-349-43549-4   ISBN 978-1-137-00812-1 (eBook)

DOI 10.1057/9781137008121

This book is printed on paper suitable for recycling and made from fully managed and sustained forest sources. Logging, pulping and manufacturing processes are expected to conform to the environmental regulations of the country of origin.

A catalogue record for this book is available from the British Library.

A catalog record for this book is available from the Library of Congress.

Typeset by MPS Limited, Chennai, India.

Contents

List of Figures and Tables viii

Acknowledgements ix

Introduction 1

1 The Mix at the Top – The Power of Psychological Diversity 5

    Global Leadership 8
    International Literacy 9
    Resilience 14
    Managing Paradoxes and Diversity 16
    Psychological Androgyny 17
    Agility and Global Nomads 20
    Team Leadership 22
    The Top Team at Barclays: Antony Jenkins, Chief Executive of Barclays 23
    What Happens in Top Teams? 26

2 Team Effectiveness – Linking Up Psychology, Culture and Strategy 29

    Observations on Team Development Initiatives 29
    The Three Levels of Team Development 31
    Level I: Governance – Basic Frameworks 32
    Level II: Skills – The Competencies 34
        Strategic skills assessment 37
        The match between executive characteristics and strategy 42
    Level III: Dynamics – Global Team Development 45
    Case Example 2.1: Global Teams at the Rockefeller Foundation 45

Case Example 2.2: Global Teams in Financial Services	47
The Link-up Between Psychology, Cultural Context and Strategy	51
Culture Shock in Teams	52

3 Global Teams — 63

Experiences of Business Leaders: Samir Brikho and Shirish Apte	63
Case 3.1: Global Team Development in Financial Services	70
Success Factors in Global Team Development	71
A Step-by-step Approach	73
The Psychological Component	78
The Cultural Component	80
The Strategic Focus	80
Top Team Health Check	83
Star Performers and How to Manage Them: Francois Curiel and Rory Sutherland	85

4 Driving Change, Growth and Innovation — 92

International Mergers – The Shock of the Alien	93
Creating a New Culture	96
Case 4.1: Accelerating a Turnaround	97
Team Governance	100
What Happens in Practice?	101
Team Diagnostics	107
Governance Workshops	110
Governance and Innovation: Thomas Geitner	112
Differences in Business Cultures	114
Resilience and Performance	118
Are Chinese Leaders More Resilient and Agile?	121
Characteristics of Chinese Leadership and Teams: Jill Lee	124
Turning around Virgin Media: Neil Berkett	126

5 Talent Over Structure — 131

Strategic Selection of Chief Executives and Top Teams	131
CEO Success Factors	134

CONTENTS

Executive Team Review	136
Case 5.1: Developing a Platform for Growth and Innovation	137
Team Dynamics	141
A Differentiated View of Business Skills, Leadership Style and Motivational Drivers	142
Assessment Methods	144
Assessment of Foreign Nationals	147
Strengths-based Assessment	152
The Innovator's DNA	154

6 Boards as Teams? 157

Governance versus Board Effectiveness	157
Board Composition	158
A Different View of Diversity	158
Board Internationalization	161
Interviews with International Board Directors	163
Gender Diversity	168
The Impact of Diversity	171
Diversity and Conflict	173
The Psychology of Boards	178
The Future of Boards – Behavioral Governance	182

Bibliography	184
Index	189

List of Figures and Tables

Figures

1.1	The Culture Shock Triangle	12
3.1	The psychological dimensions of the Culture Shock Triangle	74
4.1	The culture shock in mergers (after Oberg, 1960)	95
4.2	Team development and systemic change	99
6.1	Board comparison of Most Admired Companies (1996 versus 2010)	160

Tables

1.1	Criteria in a CEO search	8
1.2	A self-evaluation checklist on emotions, thinking and social behavior	22
2.1	Main differences between working groups and teams (following Katzenbach and Smith, 1993)	33
2.2	The key components of the psychology–context–strategy approach to global teams	52
3.1	The challenges of the global financial services team	74
3.2	Key steps to successful global team development	76
3.3	Checklist: What is your own potential as a global leader?	77
3.4	Top Team Health Check	83
4.1	Example of a development summary	109
4.2	Key findings of team profile	110
4.3	Team development agenda	110
4.4	Differences in business cultures	117

Acknowledgements

Ideas develop through stimulating and generous exchanges and I am extremely grateful to the many business leaders, colleagues and academics who inspired me. I would like to thank the following global leaders for sharing their personal experiences and leadership philosophies:

Antony Jenkins of Barclays, Samir Brikho of AMEC, Jacqueline Novogratz of Acumen Fund, Samantha Gilbert of the Rockefeller Foundation, Shirish Apte of Citi, Francois Curiel of Christie's, Rory Sutherland of Ogilvy & Mather, Thomas Geitner who was previously at Vodafone, Neil Berkett of Virgin Media, Jill Lee of ABB, Roxanne Decyk of Petrofac, Michael Harper of BBA Aviation, John McAdam of Rolls-Royce, Dr Utho Creusen of Dixons and Evelyn Havasi of Citi.

I also greatly appreciate the valuable discussions and input from the following academics and consultants: Professor Randall Peterson of London Business School, Professor Andrew Pettigrew of Oxford's Saïd Business School, Professor Chang Weining who was previously at the National University of Singapore, Professor Mark Williams of Oxford University, Professor Andrew Campbell of Ashridge Strategic Management Centre, Dr Scott Lichtenstein of Birmingham City University, Terry Lockhart of Lockhart Executive Development, with whom I originally developed the idea of a Top Team Health Check and subsequently expanded it, and Dr Chris Pierce of Global Governance Services.

My work at INSEAD's Global Leadership Centre has greatly influenced me and has always been very stimulating and enjoyable, and I am especially grateful to Professor Manfred Kets de Vries, Professor Roger Lehman, Elisabet Engellau, Jean-Claude Noel and Professor Hal Gregersen.

Following the approach of team diversity, ideas need to be implemented and I much appreciate the spirited, sensitive and effective administrative support of Christine Dunlop and the excellent computer tutorials of Charlotte Trussler at Stonehaven. My editor Tamsine O'Riordan has been encouraging and positive throughout and I am grateful for her input and for the help of Anna Keville and Josephine O'Neill. Special thanks belong to my family and friends for being tolerant and for their great support and encouragement.

Ideas develop over many years and I have been very fortunate to have met and worked with many inspiring international executives in many countries through my consulting activities – I would like to thank all the executives and clients I have worked with.

Introduction

Why do so few teams work effectively and deliver the business results they set out to achieve? Why do so many teams stay at the most basic level of collaboration (the "101" level), unable to flex their collective brainpower and problem-solving skills to beat the competition or develop new products?

With so many well-trained and business-schooled executives all over the world, this seems a puzzling result. And this is nowhere more evident than at the top of many organizations, as reflected in the collaboration of their executive teams.

Research by my former colleagues at Heidrick and Struggles, the global search firm, showed that team effectiveness at the top is low. Moreover, there is a significant disconnect between the perception of the CEO and the perception of the rest of the executive team. Chief executives always think their teams are much more effective than the rest of the team sees it (Rosen and Adair, 2007). And this pattern seems universal: whether one asks executives in Asia or the US, typical comments about the team at the top include "no one seems to agree on the strategy and we are lacking direction", "everyone is running their own show", "A and B are competing for the CEO succession and this produces tension in the team".

In my practice as a leadership consultant working with executives all over the world, the consistent question is how to build, develop and lead effective teams. And this question does not seem to abate, despite so many books on the topic. The reason lies clearly with the complexity of the topic. The psychology of an individual is complex; multiplying this by the number of team members, ideally between eight and ten, and factoring in the ever-changing dynamics of a team, we are confronted with an incomprehensible puzzle.

Nevertheless, there are ways in which to dissect and understand the puzzle, to clarify the team profile and manage the dynamics more effectively, and it is my intention to outline these in a pragmatic and applicable way with this book.

The main aim of business is to produce results and sustainable financial gains for a variety of stakeholders. Therefore, any team development needs to be imbedded in the current business context and to produce short- and long-term business results.

In order to make team development at the top accessible, I have demonstrated it with three anonymous case studies from my consulting practice. These mirror the business challenges most executives at the top of organizations or at the divisional and the functional level have to deal with:

1. How to develop global clients
2. How to turn around a stagnating business into an agile, performance-oriented and more innovative one
3. How to build the platform for fast growth.

The case studies are drawn from different industry sectors, and include teams in different locations and clients from the US to Asia. Interviews with business leaders, such as Antony Jenkins, CEO of Barclays, Samir Brikho, CEO of AMEC, Francois Curiel, Chairman of Christie's Asia, and Shirish Apte, Chairman of Citi Asia, amongst others, illustrate some of their personal challenges, whether in developed or emerging markets, and their recommendations for and learning curves with teams. The book also includes checklists and "diagnostics" which will help leaders to gauge the "health" of their own teams. The main premise is that effective team leadership is one of the most important differentiators of successful leaders, and effective team leadership can be learned and improved.

Chapter 1 shows how the criteria for effective leadership have changed, particularly as a result of the economic crisis; working in a volatile, highly interconnected global economy requires more adaptable, "new" leadership characteristics and teams that are able to use their diversity – whether national, gender or functional – to their competitive advantage. The ability to manage paradoxes, to be agile and resilient are key characteristics to adapt to constant business changes.

Chapter 2 outlines my model and pragmatic framework for building teams that produce business results by understanding

▶ INTRODUCTION 3

and taking account of psychology, cultural context and strategy. The book's core is three case studies that present paradigms of the key challenges today's executives will need to resolve throughout their careers. The case study approach will allow the reader to understand quickly what a productive approach to these different business scenarios can be and how they can apply the approach in their own organization. Checklists and summaries of key steps will make the approaches directly applicable.

Chapter 3 illustrates how to run an international business and serve global clients with a case study in financial services, integrating a team between London and New York. The "Culture Shock Triangle", which I developed in my previous book to help individual executives to adapt to international business, is extended here to understand the cornerstones of global teams. Case 3.1 then gives a step-by-step account of how the team learned to overcome cultural barriers and understand and serve its global customers better by closer collaboration. This approach led to a substantial increase in revenues and moved the team forward in the global league table. I will also include a crash course on understanding cultural differences in organizations.

How do you turn around a stagnating business? Trying to change a business, injecting some agility and making it performance oriented create resistance and tension throughout the organization. Business models are rational and we still have a mechanistic, what I call 1980s "numbers view" on how businesses operate; we assume that most executives are primarily rational and decisions are made on a financial basis. Yet, numerous boardroom clashes have long shown the emotionality of business. Often, decisions at the top are driven equally, or even more so, by the emotional make-up of the executives as by the strategy analysis of the big consulting firms.

Chapter 4 shows how a team in a large consumer business in Europe, consisting of different nationalities, accelerated organizational changes and transformed a stagnating business into a profitable one. Case 4.1 outlines steps to introduce team "essentials", such as team governance, and how to build emotional resilience and stabilize the emotional climate in a restructuring situation.

When organizations try to upscale quickly or in start-up situations, the CEO and the board often take immense efforts to have the right organizational structure. There is often an obsession with structure but less diligence is spent on analyzing the skills and styles of the executives filling the boxes in the structure. **Chapter 5** challenges the standard view of structure and roles and focuses on how to build the right platform for growth by getting the right people into the right roles and looking at the interplay of executive talent and organizational structure. Case 5.1 shows the evolving nature of a new financial services firm and raises the plea for "people over structures" when it comes to rare talent. It shows what a more objective review of management competencies, leadership style and motivational drivers can deliver. More objective reviews also help individual executives to better understand their strengths and motivation and the areas they could develop further in future. Assessing executive competencies plus a psychological assessment of leadership styles, interpersonal behavior and emotional make-up within a team are particularly powerful in this context.

The key steps and guidelines for building effective global teams, together with some diagnostic tools and benchmarking questions for leaders to take stock of the effectiveness of their teams are provided throughout the book. Interviews with business leaders in Europe, the US and Asia show some of their approaches to building effective teams, and interviews with senior executives in the not-for-profit sectors show the similarities and confluence of profit and not-for-profit sectors.

The current economic crisis, and particularly the failures of some of the major banks, has focused public attention on boards and board governance. Board diversity and board effectiveness are some of the topical areas in corporate governance discussions today and **Chapter 6** outlines the need to focus on behavioral governance and to outline a new approach to board effectiveness. It applies the team model to boards as a way to improve board effectiveness.

1 The Mix at the Top – The Power of Psychological Diversity

The mix at the top – why is it important? Is the success of organizations dependent on a single leader or is leadership at the top a team endeavor? For too many years, we bought in to the hero model of leaders: the CEO as the "white knight" parachuted in to the company when it hit troubled times or the internally groomed CEO in companies with less turbulence and longer foresight. Examples like Hewlett Packard's high-profile revolving doors cycle of CEOs should raise the question whether we have an outdated and simply inadequate idea of leadership. Equally, the economic crisis has shown that the exclusive focus on the CEO as the hero does not work. When Barclays ran into a major crisis in June 2012, the Chairman had to resign, followed by the CEO and several members of his top team. Shareholders and the public are holding entire boards of companies responsible – and not just in the financial sector – for their inability to assess risks, and the executive management teams in troubled companies are taking the blame for reckless decisions and the failure to consider the long-term consequences of decisions and the insufficient discussion of "systemic risk".

Although academics may not always be the first to spot future trends, they have questioned the "hero" leadership model for many years. Sessions at the American Management Association (one of the largest international conferences of business school academics and practitioners) targeted this issue convincingly in 2005: is our notion of hero leadership at CEO level outdated and shouldn't we look at leadership at the top in a different way, particularly at the leadership trio of Chief

Executive, Chief Financial Officer (CFO) and Chief Operating Officer (COO) – or the leadership of the entire executive team. This idea does not neglect the importance of strong individual leadership of a CEO but expands leadership to the whole executive team and focuses on the ability of the CEO to select and build high-performing teams at the top. Given the complexity of today's business through globalization and the fast pace of change, the best leaders intuitively understand the need to get the right mix of talent at the top to create a competitive advantage.

Belbin was one of the first writers to focus on the mix and the complementarity of management teams. He showed that our innate preference to recruit "people like us" is fatal in teams as it results in a group of clones that is ineffective at solving complex problems. This is nowhere more evident than in the so-called Apollo syndrome (Belbin, 1993), when a group of similar, highly intelligent experts get together: the result is a group that debates forever, engages in intellectual upmanship and does not agree on anything or get anything done. Belbin's recommendation was to put a team together comprising of people with complementary preferences, skills and behaviors. His eight team styles ranged from Chairman to Innovator to Resource Investigator. His idea was that some people like to take charge straight away whereas others like to develop new ideas and use their creativity, whilst others again love networking and are best placed to think about external and internal networks they can establish to help the team with resources, connections and alliances. Manfred Kets de Vries, the well-known leadership guru and founder of the IGLC (INSEAD's Global Leadership Centre), developed this idea of complementarity further and also differentiated eight team types, easily identifiable as "needed" capabilities at the top of organizations.

Kets de Vries' Eight Team Types (2006):

1. Strategist
2. Turnaround specialist
3. Deal-maker and negotiator
4. Business builder/entrepreneur
5. Innovator

6. Efficiency expert
7. People developer
8. Communicator/stage manager.

Of course, very few of us fall neatly into one or the other category, as most of us have preferences for two or three styles and hopefully also abilities and skills in different areas.

In essence, business leaders have to ask themselves whether they have enough strategists and lateral thinkers on the team, supported by executives with strong operational excellence, networking and marketing skills. As many studies have shown, it is the mix of different backgrounds, skills, thinking and behavior that marks a high-performance team.

And it is this diversity in the broadest sense that characterizes effective global teams, as we will see in research studies and practical examples throughout this book.

However, diverse teams do not always perform better than less diverse or homogenous teams. It entirely depends on the complexity of the challenge. For example, with non-complex problems, homogenous teams perform better. Here, a diverse team may simply get distracted by too much lateral thinking. In complex challenges, however, as in most international business situations, diverse or heterogeneous teams produce much better solutions than homogenous teams, as shown by Gratton and Erickson (2007). In their study, teams consisting of men and women developed more creative solutions than all-male or all-female teams. The positive effect of diversity also applies to company boards. In a study on board diversity, I found that the boards of the Most Admired Companies in the UK's FTSE 100 group (as evaluated and ranked by the magazine *Management Today*) had more diverse boards in the broadest sense: they had more board directors with international experience, greater functional diversity, a broader diversity in age and more women on their boards (Marx, 1998). If we just look at the very topical issue of gender diversity, we are receiving more and more data showing that gender-diverse boards and the performance of companies are positively correlated.

Commenting on the topic in Britain, one UK Chairman remarked: "We were an all-male board – typical of the 'stale, pale and male' category. Once the first women joined, the dynamics of the board clearly changed; not only were we more polite with each other but, more importantly, we started to discuss things more." The argument at board level is similar to the argument in teams: we need different experiences and skills, and to have psychologically or cognitively diverse boards that can analyze complex business scenarios, challenge one another and develop productive strategies to deal with the massive challenges most businesses face today and in future.

The economic crisis has sparked an important question about effective leadership for the future.

Global Leadership

Through my search and consulting activities, I have a privileged insight into the challenges of leaders. Day to day, I see the complexity of having the right talent in the right roles, matching talent to the culture and strategy of the organization and managing the dynamics of a team. I will address all these aspects of developing executive teams using case studies as examples. But before understanding a whole group of individual leaders representing functions or business divisions, we need to understand what the "new" leadership characteristics look like – what capabilities are necessary to be successful in adapting to the global volatility in a resilient way? The criteria

Table 1.1 Criteria in a CEO search

- Excellent industry track record in a well-established international business
- Proven ability as a strategic business builder, with entrepreneurial orientation and substantial record in growing businesses
- Strong negotiation skills
- Excellent operational experience, combined with progressive customer service strategies
- High numeracy and comfortable with risk-taking to take advantage of business opportunities
- Substantial international work experience, ideally also in emerging markets
- Experience in international acquisitions and their integration
- Excellent leadership skills, ability to motivate, professionalism, influence, judgement, integrity and emotional intelligence
- Sophisticated and culturally sensitive interpersonal skills
- High drive and motivation to grow a business, proactive and positive approach.

applied in the search for a Divisional CEO of a conglomerate are given in Table 1.1 and illustrate some of these "new" attributes. This is just a snapshot of the entire list of "wanted characteristics" and shows that most companies expect superman or superwomen at the top. The differentiation between prior experience and success, business competencies and psychological leadership characteristics is obvious – an effective taxonomy to understand and manage these is less so. The number of boards failing to make the right selection decisions testifies to this. In consulting, one often focuses on the following skills or competencies:

▷ Strategic thinking ability
▷ Operational effectiveness (turnaround, growth, experience)
▷ Team leadership
▷ Customer and client orientation
▷ International capability
▷ Problem-solving
▷ Creativity
▷ Stakeholder management
▷ Relationship skills
▷ Motivation and drive
▷ Emotional resilience.

We can calibrate these business competencies through structured interviews and, in searches, through careful references. The above candidate specification also shows how the demographic variables of leaders have changed over the last decade. We find more and more global CEOs at the top of large organizations.

International Literacy

> Samir Brikho is the Chief Executive of AMEC plc, one of the world's largest engineering, project management and consultancy companies, with over 29 000 employees, and offices and projects in over 40 countries. AMEC has major operating centres in the UK and the Americas and is one of the largest British companies and part of the FTSE 100 Index.

> Samir Brikho's profile is a good example of the "new" leader: Lebanese by birth, his family moved to Sweden, where he was brought up and educated. He has an engineering degree and a Master of Science in Thermal Technology from the Royal Institute of Technology in Stockholm, with Advanced Leadership Courses at several international business schools (INSEAD and Stanford); he held a succession of senior executive positions with ABB, including becoming a member of their executive team, before being appointed Chief Executive of AMEC in 2006. He has lived and worked in numerous countries, including Sweden, UAE, Saudi Arabia, Switzerland, Germany, Belgium, France and, since 2006, the UK. He also speaks five languages fluently: Swedish, Arabic, English, German and French.

International literacy is one of the key features of the new leader. International literacy is the ability to move between cultures, understand and work with the differences in cultures and deal with customers and business partners effectively. This shift towards greater international capability is nowhere more evident than in the career profiles of CEOs at the top of large multinationals. Having considered the career profiles of the largest 100 UK companies by market capitalization (FTSE 100 companies) over the last 15 years, the pattern is pretty clear cut. Whereas in 1996, 42 percent of CEOs of the FTSE 100 companies had international experience, by 2007 this figure had jumped to 67 percent (Marx, 1997, 2008). And we see another jump in this figure post-economic crisis. When I analyzed the profiles of CEOs appointed to FTSE 100 companies between 2008 and 2010, as many as 75 percent had, as in Samir Brikho's case, spent considerable time working abroad.

This picture is completely different on the other side of the Atlantic. My transatlantic comparison of chief executives showed that Fortune 100 CEOs had significantly less overseas experience compared to their UK counterparts: only 33 percent of Fortune 100 CEOs had international experience earlier in their career.

British companies also are often led by foreign-born chief executives; for example, Marjorie Scardino, the now outgoing US-born CEO of Pearson plc and the first woman CEO of a FTSE 100 company, or Paul Polman, the Dutch CEO of Unilever. A similar internationalization is taking place in boards, as we will see in Chapter 6.

1 ▶ THE MIX AT THE TOP

The transatlantic comparison of chief executives' profiles raised a debate on both sides of the Atlantic about whether international experience – defined in my research as having lived or worked abroad for a minimum of one year – is necessary to develop international literacy and to run a global company.

So what determines the ability to understand global economic factors, operate in different geographic regions, and understand the cultural differences of employees and customers? In other words, what makes a global leader?

In my book *Breaking Through Culture Shock: What you need to succeed in international business* (2001), I argued that international effectiveness requires a deeper understanding, exposure and "confrontation" with the "other" culture. It is part of a longer term personal development rather than the number of airmiles one clocks up on international flights.

Succession management in multinationals focuses on senior executives' international experience and capability, their understanding of global business and of global clients. Many organizations try to select leaders who are culturally sensitive, have a flexible approach, good interaction skills and the confidence to deal with complex and unpredictable business scenarios. Development assessments of the top 100 or 150 executives in multinationals focus on these capabilities more and more. As summarized in my article "Developing Global Leaders" (Marx, 2004), global leaders have to deal with the three main dimensions of culture shock – emotions, thinking and social skills, the Culture Shock Triangle (Marx, 2001).

On the basis of my research on the personal and professional experiences of over 200 international executives from far reaching geographies, it became clear that if we want to be effective on a global basis, we have to break through the culture shock that confronts us every day in business, whether we are responsible for expanding a business in South East Asia or dealing with Asian and South American customers from our headquarters in the UK, the US or Germany. Whereas living and working in a different country certainly facilitates this development and makes it acutely necessary, anyone can develop better global leadership, focusing on the three dimensions of the Culture Shock Triangle.

The international challenges in these dimensions are described in Figure 1.1 below:

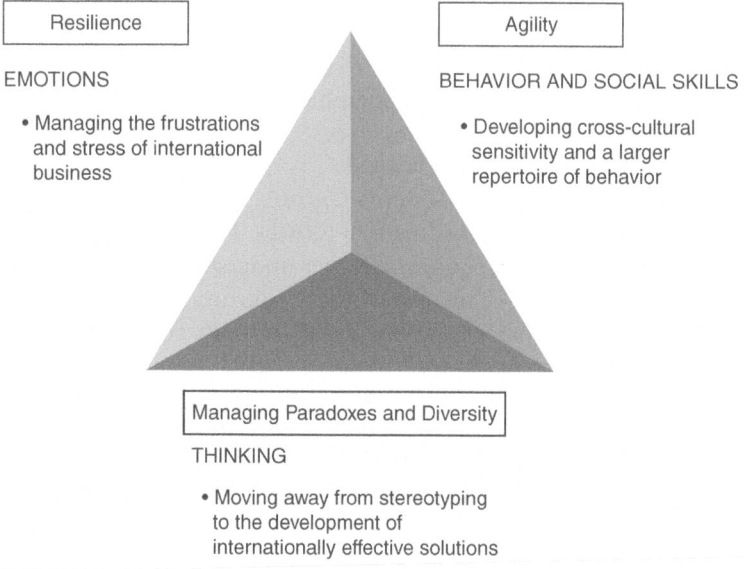

Figure 1.1 **The Culture Shock Triangle**

This psychological framework has concrete practical application and can be used in developing individual executives and international teams.

Some examples for the application of the Culture Shock Triangle in a wide range of executive challenges are as follows:

▷ Board Effectiveness: accelerating the board induction of a continental European executive to the board of a British FTSE 100 company
▷ Merger Integration: advising the managing director of a French/British merger on how to build better collaboration in his international team
▷ Understanding Global Clients: improving the understanding of the global customer base of a team in a global telecommunications company

1 ▶ THE MIX AT THE TOP

▷ International Growth Plans: advising an international investment bank on the structure and roles of its executive team
▷ Accelerating business turnarounds in different businesses through international team development.

Imagine you are sitting in your office in London working on an update on a complex global consulting assignment with a client in Asia. The project has been going well and you have an excellent track record and long-standing relationship with the client. Yet, you have just found out that the client is thinking of switching consultancies. At first, you are probably angry, a bit confused and maybe even feel "betrayed". You don't understand what is going on and sitting in your office five thousand miles away from the client does not help. This may be unusual client behavior in Europe, but is it "normal" client behavior in some parts of Asia? What is "normal"? What is the most effective response to the situation?

One could say, "three simple steps": first of all, keep calm and then, if you have not done so already, check your assumptions and find out more about how this client and clients in the region operate, and then get advice from someone in the region on the most effective response. This may be to think of all possible next steps and how to react, as in scenario planning, but also to leave things quite open. Looking at myself, the "German in me" would probably like to pick up the phone and find out exactly what is going on and what the client's plans are, the "British in me" would try to deal with the ambiguity and let it run for a while, and probably try to understand more about Asia and take a diplomatic approach that aims at preserving the relationship in the long run.

This simple scenario shows the need to manage the emotional side of international business – we often experience greater mood fluctuations than when working locally because of the greater unpredictability involved. Similarly, on the thinking side, when we find out that our "normal" way of doing things does not work, we have to challenge our assumptions as to what works in business and become more creative in finding solutions (more of this in Chapter 3). In relation to social skills, we need to "upscale" our behavior and learn the behavioral rules of our foreign counterparts. As we shall see in Chapter 3, these "rules" differ enormously, from the expression of emotion to nonverbal communication, as in eye contact and physical proximity in interactions.

Resilience

Observing senior executives and their teams over the last four years of the economic crisis, what strikes me most is that global leaders are able to "hold" tension in all dimensions of the Culture Shock Triangle and, more positively, know how to use the tensions in each of the areas effectively.

Closing business deals brings mixed emotions of excitement, enjoyment and frustration. We need the awareness and confidence to recognize these emotions, accept them as normal and manage them effectively. The expectation of emotional rollercoasters and managing the "emotional stakes" of global business are key features in effective international leaders. Regarding the cognitive/thinking side, effective leaders show an ability and often preference to deal with the complexity of global business, its ambiguity and the risk they are operating in. The inability of the big banks to manage risk has been clearly exposed in the current financial crisis – it has also shown the tendency to "delegate" risk management to a specific function or technical director without sufficient systemic risk discussion on the executive team level or board level. For executives who like maximum clarity, predictability and black-and-white solutions, international business is difficult. For those who like and prefer complexity, the economic turbulence provides huge opportunities.

The last couple of years since the onset of the economic crisis have been an emotional rollercoaster for most people, and I do not mean just business or "the West". Stress levels in many places are at an unprecedented high and the prescription of anti-depressants in the UK has increased by 40 percent in the last four years. Stress-induced illness and absenteeism in the workplace create gigantic losses for business, apart from the more important human tragedies involved. And the very top of organizations is affected by stress.

It is a brave decision of the CEO and the board to disclose these effects and the personal challenges of individuals publicly. It also has sparked a debate about our expectations of top leaders and chief executives. In September 2010, after battling the financial crisis in their respective banks for over two years, four highly respected executives of major European banks announced their retirement and newspaper articles suggested they were tired out overseeing banks through one of the biggest financial crises.

In the last four years, the resilience of chief executives has been tested to the limit. Resilience or emotional robustness is a defining characteristic in many areas: highly successful people in all walks of life have higher energy and a greater drive to succeed; they show more perseverance in the face of obstacles and bounce back from failures swiftly. Most chief executives I know have all the above characteristics plus a capacity for work that supersedes the average person's. A 63-year-old CEO of a trans-Atlantic business frequently comes back on the overnight "Red Eye" from New York to London, goes straight to the office in the morning and works a full day. Yet, we also know from executive participants of business schools that many senior executives show a high stress vulnerability and not the level of resilience we would expect.

Moreover, 360° feedback (direct feedback from an employee's subordinates, peers and superiors, as well as self-evaluation) data shows that others often see leaders as much more resilient than the leaders see themselves – executives often admit a vulnerability and feel less prepared to deal with the pressures or do not feel they have the right work/life balance. Whereas most executives are aware of their physical fitness, the emotional fitness and resilience of leaders is hardly discussed. Indeed, the assumption is that business is rational and unemotional – yet, "on the ground", we see that business is highly emotional at the top and these emotional "high stakes" have become more evident in the present rollercoaster of Europe and other parts of the world. The fact that business is often not at all rational and many business decisions are based on irrational and often unconscious biases has been best shown by the Nobel Prize winner Daniel Kahnemann in his ground-breaking book *Thinking, Fast and Slow* (Kahnemann, 2011).

Managing Paradoxes and Diversity

Global leadership requires us to "hold" and then reconcile incompatible ideas and to manage *paradoxes*. When F. Scott Fitzgerald described the mark of a first-rate intelligence as "the ability to hold two opposed ideas in the mind at the same time, and still retain the ability to function", he probably did not intend to describe tomorrow's leaders. Yet, it probably has been a feature of successful leaders throughout time – the need for this ability has simply become more evident in the current crisis, as it has forced us to reflect very seriously whether our view of leaders has been adequate in the widest sense.

Marx and Tappin identified the ability to deal with paradoxes as a key criterion of future leaders. We often select future leaders on their ability to think strategically and to develop a vision for the company. However, strategic thinking is not sufficient on its own: "it needs to be complemented by a focus on operational results and the ability to switch fluidly from long-term to short-term thinking, from helicopter view to operational details, from cost saving to expansion and growth. The flexibility to handle this potential paradox and deal with seemingly incompatible extremes characterizes the top executives of the future" (Marx and Tappin, 2006, p.95). The ability to reconcile the pressure for short-term profits with the building of long-term success and sustainability is probably the prime example most executives recognize immediately. Leadership and businesses that can reconcile the short- and long-term profit tension through the right structure, governance and, most importantly, culture are the ones that will ultimately be sustainable. A good example in the UK is the John Lewis Partnership, a retailer owned by an employee trust and which has thrived throughout the economic crisis in contrast to many of its competitors.

The ability to reconcile contradictions can also be seen as the need to balance the interest of internal and external stakeholders. Think about the cult of the CEO of the 1990s – the charismatic personality who was media-friendly – and compare this with those internally focused chief executives described by Jim Collins in *Good to Great* (2001) who shun the public light, are internally focused and concentrate on long-term legacies of their companies.

In a recent article on "Star Performers", Manfred Kets de Vries suggests that "stars' paradoxical behavior is what makes them so successful" (2012, p.173). Referring to Carl Jung's concept of the need for human beings to resolve the conflict of dualities and the tension this produces, Kets de Vries gives an erudite description of the many cognitive opposites that the star performer seems to be able to reconcile. The opposites of analytical (convergent) and creative (divergent) thinking, of reflection and action, and of optimism and realism.

Of course, all these characteristics are extremely evident in the make-up of diverse teams. Yet, we are hardly aware of these opposites "raging within us", except in moments of crisis at professional and personal crossroads. Hence, a greater awareness of our preferred styles and the way we integrate these opposites is necessary before we even try to understand the opposites in teams and to find sensitive and sensible ways to develop complex, diverse teams – whether these consist of different nationalities, gender, age ranges, functional backgrounds, and personalities and skills – i.e. managing the diversity in teams.

Only if we understand these opposites and "the way they play out" in ourselves, are we able to recognize and understand them in others and "use" these opposites creatively in a team that will ultimately deliver business results.

In some ways, our business model has been shaken up by the financial crisis. To be blunt, the 1980s static, data-obsessed model of individuals as human capital – to be counted, scored and managed like a balance sheet – has not been entirely successful. It assumed a predictability of business and behavior that is simply not valid anymore. The interdependency of national and global markets has made this more than obvious. Governments, whole industry sectors and many companies are often primarily focused on bringing in more regulation and controls, without questioning whether we need to change our view of the basic parameters of business.

Psychological Androgyny

The need to integrate opposites and to "use" opposites is well demonstrated in the concept of *psychological androgyny*, spearheaded in the 1970s in the psychological research of Sandra Bem. Building on Jung's concept of the female within the male psyche (anima) and the male within the female psyche (animus), and the related characteristics of active/passive and rational/emotional, she created the term psychological androgyny (derived from the Greek words Andros, male, and Gumne, female). Bem developed a personality questionnaire to measure a previously nebulous concept and started systematic research on wellbeing and adaptation. She demonstrated in her research that a combination of masculine and feminine dispositions is more adaptive than stereotypical extremes. Bad news for the alpha male and beta female! Other studies show the positive effect of psychological androgyny on creativity and emotional intelligence. In the business world, sporadic studies show that leaders with both masculine and feminine traits are best at producing a climate for innovation (Solberg, 2008). Steve Jobs' interest in dancing, calligraphy, Buddhism and meditation illustrates the integration of diverse interests/activities with producing commercially successful products and astonishing business results. Apple at this point is still the most valuable company in the US.

In his book *A Whole New Mind*, Daniel Pink has made one of the most cogent and detailed arguments for the pursuit of highly lateral interests that engage, challenge and expand our way of thinking. As Pink explains, whereas the last decades have focused on producing highly analytical minds, able to understand and manipulate the most complex balance sheets, the future belongs to different minds. "What is in greatest demand today is an analytical synthesis – seeing the big picture, crossing boundaries, and being able to combine disparate pieces into an interesting new whole" (Pink, 2005, p.66). In other words, Pink advocates that the "left brain era" is over in favor of the right brainers; that is, in today's uncertain world, the analytical thinking of the left brain is probably less effective compared to the right brain's ability to synthesize, seeing the bigger picture, empathize and create meaning.

He outlines six specific ways to develop this new mind and we may wonder why, following his argument, more business schools are not focusing on developing the right hemisphere, beyond the well-established courses in improving emotional intelligence in leaders, self-awareness, knowledge and impact of one's leadership behavior.

The leadership courses at business schools are clearly making a difference in developing a whole new mind. One of the professors at INSEAD's Global Leadership Centre uses a catching image in his introduction of leadership development programs. He tells the class of executives that observing them entering the classroom in the morning, he could see "the heavily left-tilted heads of the left-brain thinkers, which he hoped to balance out with the development of softer skills by the end of the program". These leadership courses are increasingly popular and, for example, the longer development program for the Executive MBAs often shows significant changes in leadership behavior. But could they be complemented by other modules to "create a symphony or meaning" following Pink?

Relating these ideas to the context of international business and international teams, I wonder whether the so-called collectivistic societies in Asia or the Middle East are much better prepared to deal with the future than our individualistic and highly analytical world in the US, UK or many parts of Northern Europe? Are more people-oriented societies, as the collectivistic cultures (that are more synergistic and context-oriented), more ready for the future than our individualistic thinking that is sequential and task-oriented? I will look at this question more closely in Chapters 3 and 4.

Psychoanalysis and psychology have always been highly interested in the personality dimension of androgyny. Poets and writers have consistently commented that a "great mind is androgynous", as in creative. This holding of intellectual tension – of staying fluid whilst being differentiated in observation and judgement and in admitting to the changing of views while exploring all options – is probably best illustrated in the essay writing of Michel de Montaigne (1533–93). De Montaigne understood how to reconcile the abstract with deeply personal observations, blending philosophical reflections with personal experiences. His writings show the wanderings of the mind and the superiority of divergent thinking in understanding the most complex human and morally challenging situations. It also shows the role of ambiguity of many situations and how a fast, "black and white" and determined way of thinking and decision-making is often inadequate for complex situations.

Yet, most businesses in the Western hemisphere are still preoccupied with the assertive leader who makes fast decisions, is action oriented and relatively "black and white". The focus is on short-term results and high task-orientation. Psychological androgyny could also potentially be defined as integrating task and people orientation. The holding of tensions may actually be characteristic of the more relation-oriented cultures like the Middle East and Asia, where the development of strong relationships and getting the task achieved are often seen as synonymous; the general business approach is often non-linear and processes and frameworks not as important as keeping things flexible.

Agility and Global Nomads

An adaptive leader knows when to be tough and assertive and when to use a more consultative, coaching and softer approach.

The interpersonal dimension of integrating and balancing extremes includes:

▷ When to be team oriented versus self-sufficient
▷ When to be socially active and network versus periods of withdrawal
▷ When to listen and when to act/close off discussions
▷ When to be culturally adaptive and when to be consistent with your national identity.

Similar to the expansion of thinking, we are essentially looking for an expansion of our "behavioral repertoire", without jeopardizing some fundamental ways in which we do things. This is also reflected in the question of national identity and being an internationalist or having a trans-national self.

There is a growing group of global nomads of international high-achievers who seem "at home in the world", crossing national and industry boundaries easily and defying the need for a prescriptive national identity of any kind. David Adjaye, the African British architect designing the Smithsonian National Museum of African American Culture and History, is a good example of this group. Asked by a journalist whether he feels more African than British, he commented, "Well look at me, I am obviously African and I have an African soul but I can't deny my Britishness either – I am both these things. But I don't think my generation need a passport to define their nationality" (*Financial Times*, 16 September 2012). Spending time between Europe, India and the Middle East as well as the US and South America, his view is "migration has changed, it's not what it used to be, after the Smithsonian, I might spend five years in Africa or Asia."

This pattern of a "globetrotting plutocracy" is well documented by Chrystia Freeland in her research on the "Rise and Fall of the New Global Elite" (2011). Studying the Wall Street plutocrats or Russian billionaires, she observes that "the cultural ties that bind the super-rich to everyone else are fraying from both ends…" (2011, p.10).

We are seeing a similar pattern in the chief executive community, with one-third of the UK's FTSE 100 CEOs being foreign nationals (Marx, 2008). Chief executive profiles are predictive as to how the younger high-flyers will organize their careers in future. The advantage of these global nomads is that they are well able to maneuver the international business landscape and have the knowledge and openness to be successful in complex business settings. The concerns which Freeland rightly outlines are that they see themselves "increasingly as a global community, distinguished in their unique talents and above such parochial concerns as national identities…" (2011, p.10). Or in other words, these are business elites that are too far removed from their communities' concerns and too far removed from the people they are leading. If we are *internationalists* transcending national boundaries, what is the effect on our national identity and on our core values? How do we juggle the tension between formative national experiences and the developing of an international identity? Or to put it differently, how do we achieve consistency in behavior whilst being adaptive to different cultural settings and dealing with a diversity of colleagues or clients?

As this chapter has suggested, traditional leadership models (pre-economic crisis) were based on a strong predictability of business where financial forecasts and strong financial controls, together with good strategic planning, would often ensure the desired business results. The economic unpredictability post-Lehman, together with the greater interdependency of global markets, requires leaders to stretch their capabilities and ways of doing things. This different level of complexity requires more synthesis, creativity and the ability to integrate extremes.

Table 1.2 A self-evaluation checklist on emotions, thinking and social behavior

Emotions and drive
- Confidence versus apprehension and worrying
- Optimism versus realism
- Energy/drive versus balance
- Emotional display/passion versus calmness, particularly in crisis

Thinking
- Strategic thinking versus pragmatic/operational orientation
- Long-term sustainability versus short-term profits
- Ambiguity versus predictability and control
- Traditionalism versus innovation

Social behavior
- Introverted versus extravert behavior
- Task-orientation versus people-orientation
- Empathy versus ruthlessness
- Team-orientation versus self-sufficiency

Doing a short evaluation of yourself, where do you see yourself in juggling the extremes that global business demands?

Team Leadership

Going down the list in Table 1.2, it probably becomes evident that we may have some dimensions in which we juggle these extremes very well whereas in other dimensions we find it more difficult to integrate the paradoxes and need to rely on the power of a diverse team. Understanding our preferences in these dimensions helps us understand the diversity in teams and to "leverage" diversity in its broadest sense.

Effective team leadership is understanding the key criteria for business now and in the future, having a realistic self-evaluation and focusing on the development of these characteristics in the team and throughout the business. The effective CEO of the future shows superior team leadership, also expressed as a cooperative leader.

This view is also supported by Professor Randall Peterson of London Business School, who is an expert on teams. Exploring the impact of the competitive versus cooperative leader on teams, he notes that "the strengths of the cooperative style are found in the higher likelihood that this kind of group will make superior decisions because they have pooled their expertise" (Peterson, 2007, p.75). And, "to be successful, Chief Executives and senior management teams must be equipped to cope with unpredictability. This favors the more cooperative approach" (Peterson, 2007, p.76). But how do leaders manage all this in real life? The following interview with Antony Jenkins, Chief Executive of Barclays, gives essential insights into his approach to cultural change through cooperation and team leadership.

The Top Team at Barclays: Antony Jenkins, Chief Executive of Barclays

Antony Jenkins was appointed Group Chief Executive of Barclays in August 2012. The press at the time suggested that the " 'Nice guy Antony Jenkins' appointment" indicated the demise of the "Masters of the Universe" in banking.

The following interview with Antony Jenkins captures his approach to culture change, leadership from the top and his focus on teams and collaboration.

The first 100 days – the start of culture change

The Plan

In some ways, I was already prepared for the current cultural change of Barclays. In the run-up to the financial crisis, it became obvious to me that the industry needed to change. The crisis made this much more urgent as it became clear that the industry had lost the concept of serving its stakeholders.

In my previous roles as Head of Barclaycard and Head of Retail Banking at Barclays, I had already worked on the concept of serving stakeholders and had advocated for change within Barclays. The events of the Libor crisis in the summer of 2012, including my predecessor's departure, forced a complete re-think for Barclays. My transition to the CEO role started in late August when I identified the key elements for my "Transform Program" whilst I was interviewing with the Board. I knew we had good businesses and we had good people, but somewhere along the line things had gone wrong. I remember I was on a flight to New York when I put together my first notes on the strategy. On that flight, I developed the three strategic cornerstones of the culture change required: (1) achieving a turnaround (2) returning acceptable numbers and (3) ensuring sustainable forward momentum. As I am not good at PowerPoint, I simply went to the Board with a "two-pager" and described the main ideas and implementation plans. Once appointed, I built ten different work streams to deliver these ideas, with the ultimate objective of making Barclays the "Go-To Bank".

The Actions

Stakeholder engagement

I began by engaging very intensely with our stakeholders, i.e. the top 30 to 40 shareholders, key government figures and the regulators. The first phase was spending time listening to the different stakeholders and seeking to understand what was on their mind. I then started articulating our plan and how we would update on the progress against the plan. As a consequence, the relationship with these different sets of stakeholders is now much better.

People agenda

Internally, people were more open and perhaps less skeptical than I expected. They immediately bought in to the overall vision of becoming the "Go-To Bank". Barclays had never had a clear, unified culture and therefore we needed to be explicit about having the right values and the right behaviors. So we agreed a common purpose and values to underpin it; for example, one of the core values we have agreed is respect. If we look at respect, collaboration is a key behavior and key for cultural change. Collaboration has always been valued but it was not widespread enough and there was never a real commercial imperative to drive collaboration.

Now, we have a clear commercial imperative for collaboration and this is reflected in our Balanced Scorecard and collaboration becomes a driver of performance assessment and reward.

Selection and development of the executive team

Leadership creates culture and culture creates performance. We are introducing specific training for the top 150 executives on what the role of a senior leader is at Barclays. Culture change is manageable and can be implemented if you have the right diagnostics and the right management actions.

I immediately made some significant changes to the executive committee and promoted two of my former key executives, the Head of Barclaycard and the Head of Retail Bank, to the executive team. It was the right thing to do, given the significance of these two businesses in our Group. I also created a new role of Group Head of Operations and Technology. This also resulted in an internal promotion, after carefully reviewing the external market. The team is not complete yet – we are currently recruiting a Group HR Director, a CFO and a General Counsel. I believe both in bringing in more talent and in priority talent.

Collaboration at the top

A high-performing team has two characteristics: it is effective at problem-solving, and members are not selfish; it means everyone is able to focus on the bigger issues. The second point has been a challenge traditionally. In selecting top executives, we traditionally recruited domain expertise and a high degree of intellect. In future, I think that the ability to collaborate will become the biggest driver of change. If we want Barclays to succeed, collaboration at the top will be essential to make the change. However, I also recognize that sometimes the collaboration is at odds with other drivers. For example, we want to have self-starters who are autonomous, but we want them to be highly collaborative.

In the executive committee, everybody needs to step up and operate outside their functional or business niche. We want collective problem-solving and we carry out careful assessments to make sure we have the right leadership characteristics. Then there is a question around how we work together. When I was Head of the Retail Bank, I built a much closer team and organized for enough informal meetings where we talked about how we wanted to operate as a team. We changed the agenda for our meetings and had more cross-business discussions.

To develop an effective team means also being prepared for effective conflict management. Conflict is often seen as a bad thing and there is a lot of conflict aversion at the top level. However, I believe that conflict is not necessarily a bad thing – the worst thing is to ignore it. One has to have a clear way to resolve it, as it will otherwise make any fast decision-making impossible.

Personal challenges in progressing to Group Chief Executive

On reflection, there were probably three areas that were very different to my former roles and where I needed to step up. The first area was

> the number of complex problems landing on your desk. The velocity of this is intense, requiring effectiveness and good time management. Secondly, I was prepared for media exposure, but probably not for the extent of media scrutiny. The third area is the interaction with the Board. Although I had presented to the Board before and knew how to engage with the Board, as the Group Chief Executive you need to find a way to respond respectfully to everyone whilst creating coherence.
>
> The Chairman is extremely important in this transition and I have been very fortunate to have Sir David Walker as Chairman, who has written extensively on corporate governance issues and has a clear philosophy of creating effective boards.

The interview with Antony Jenkins shows the challenges of culture change and how a Group CEO addresses these in the face of strong public scrutiny. That this CEO is serious about the implementation of cultural change was reinforced in news coverage in January 2013 indicating that Antony Jenkins told the bank's 140,000 employees to sign up to the new code of conduct or leave the bank, and that he and the Chairman, Sir David Walker, stated their commitment to reward those who adhere to Barclays' values as opposed to exclusively focusing on short-term profits.

What Happens in Top Teams?

In business practice, we often find that team collaboration is at a rudimentary level, as suggested by the following indicators:

▷ Team meetings that do not allow time for a real discussion
▷ A short-term focus where urgent issues overpower the important ones
▷ No clear framework for decision-making
▷ Very little joint problem-solving.

Whilst there is no "one size fits all" approach to team development, there are classic challenges any leader needs to tackle, from selecting the right people to having good team processes in place and trying to solve emerging business problems as a group.

The unrealistic perceptions of leaders

My former colleagues Rich Rosen and Fred Adair at Heidrick and Struggles analyzed the findings of a large-scale study, with the University of Southern California's Centre for Effective Organizations. It gives an excellent glimpse of the state of top management teams (TMTs) of large organizations, and the unrealistic perception of team effectiveness by chief executives. These are some of the findings:

1. Surveying 60 top executives from Fortune 500 companies, only 6 percent reported that the executives at the top of the organization, what the US calls the C-suite, are a well-integrated team (Rosen and Adair, 2007)
2. Chief executives consistently overrated the effectiveness and performance of their top management teams; the executive team gives much less favorable ratings of its effectiveness. For example, in a global survey of 124 CEOs and 579 senior executives, 52 percent of executives rated the team as performing poorly in areas such as leading change or innovation, whereas only 28 percent of CEOs saw problems in these areas
3. Only 42 percent of the Human Resources executives suggested that the "ability to work in a team" was considered when externally recruiting or internally promoting executives to the top of organizations (Rosen and Adair, 2008).

This is one of the few recent large-scale studies looking at the situation of executive teams or top management. What are effective and practical models to achieve better team effectiveness?

Given that the concept of team development is often seen as nebulous and not well understood, I decided to address it in the context of specific business challenges that most leaders need to tackle in their business career – universal challenges in all sectors.

The three main business challenges addressed in this book are:

▷ How to develop an international team and serve global clients (Chapter 3)
▷ How to turnaround a stagnant, bureaucratic business into a performance-oriented one (Chapter 4)
▷ How to build a platform for fast growth and innovation, whether in a corporate or more entrepreneurial setting (Chapter 5).

2 Team Effectiveness – Linking Up Psychology, Culture and Strategy

Observations on Team Development Initiatives

Most senior executives have at some point participated in a team development exercise. The largest organizations spend hundreds of thousands of pounds or dollars every year developing their teams, at every level of the organization. A senior researcher with one of the world's leading pharmaceutical companies recently sighed "another one of my boss's team development off-sites is coming up, at another five-star hotel, flying everyone in and probably having another 'carrying poles around the garden exercise' as part of it." Despite this joking reference, he also said that the team off-sites had produced a much better glue, which helped a closer international research collaboration.

Nevertheless, the exact effects of team development are rarely analyzed or objectively demonstrated. The term team development is nebulous and vague, as it can describe anything from outbound, military style, physical team-bonding exercises to in-depth psychological development with behavioral feedback to each member of the team. My observations from practice are as follows:

▷ Despite the many forms of and approaches to team development, we often do not know what works best, if it works at all, how it works and what type of development we should aim for in our own teams
▷ Given the abundance of business school courses, books and direct exposure to different forms of team development, most

executives still do not know some of the basic elements of team work or have a framework that helps them in pulling a team together
▷ In assessments of competencies of senior executives, team leadership inevitably comes out as one of the lowest ranking competencies as opposed to the harder business skills of operational effectiveness or customer orientation
▷ Team development initiatives become rarer the higher we go up the organization, which may be caused by the discrepancy between the CEO's perception of the effectiveness of his or her team and the team's perception (as we have seen in Chapter 1)
▷ Many senior executives only reach the top because of their highly competitive, single-minded and often individualistic streak and are then all of a sudden expected to be a team player. This can be particularly hard when several team members are vying for the CEO's position.

Whereas in the past, we have looked at the executive team as a group of functional leaders, coming together, updating each other and running their respective operations or business divisions, the need for a team approach for the success of a business (using the collective brainpower of the executive team) has never been more evident than right now.

When I asked Samir Brikho, the highly successful international CEO of AMEC, how his leadership behavior has changed and developed over time, he commented:

> Reflecting on myself over the last ten years, I would say that I learnt to listen, tolerate, respect, sense and feel. Whereas before, I had to believe that the solution is within me and I would give the answers to all the questions that arise, I now see my role to ask the right questions and get the solutions from someone else. I try to ask the right questions to help the team to crystallize the issue and thereby facilitate the solution. Am I advisor or coach? I see my role being to inspire people, giving them the confidence and tools to achieve and deliver excellence against stretch targets.

The CEO as the Chair and Advisor coordinating and coaching the team to find the right solutions and empowering it to use its collective knowledge, experience and creativity is seen by many experts as the ideal style of an effective leader – as opposed to the traditional, hierarchical model of giving orders, controlling and leaving little space and time for the team to explore. Samir Brikho also observes another benefit of his own development as a leader in relation to his personal life: "There is also the risk of being prescriptive, giving solutions in your professional life if you transfer this to your private life. For example, your partner or child may ask you a question in order to have a conversation about it and you simply give a solution and tell them what to do." Rather than being complacent, this CEO also knows the need to stretch himself continuously, trying to learn new things: "I give myself the challenge to learn something every day. It is important to stretch myself and to do something every day that one is slightly scared of; some risk-taking is necessary to continue learning."

Most executives, whether at the middle or the top level of an organization, would probably benefit from knowing different frameworks to effective team development, not theoretical but very practical frameworks that illustrate solutions to different team scenarios and that are based on well-proven techniques.

The Three Levels of Team Development

In my consulting work, I differentiate between the following three different levels of team development – these can be applied in isolation or in combination.

Levels of team development

Level I: *Governance* – basic frameworks and recommendations to pull the team together
Level II: *Skills* – the competencies and attributes needed
Level III: *Dynamics* – global team development: aligning the team to strategic objectives, creating focus, collaboration, momentum and adaptability to changing markets.

Level I (Governance) is important for business heads or team leaders who want to develop solid corporate governance or frameworks. It is useful for executives who know they have already the right team and skills but want to get traction swiftly and have a coordinated approach.

Level II (Skills) is for CEOs or leaders who are building a new operation, restructuring an existing one, or expanding or internationalizing their companies. They need to ask themselves whether they have the right skill sets to achieve the targets and whether they have the right structure for the organization.

Level III (Dynamics) goes beyond the building blocks of having the right people competencies, structure and governance, and focuses on "making the team work" and, most importantly, making it *agile* to adapt to different economic scenarios. It focuses on developing the right dynamics, energy and resilience of the top team. This includes a more sophisticated psychological understanding of the make-up of the team, the motivation of the team, its emotions and dynamics. It also focuses on a better understanding of the interplay between culture (organizational and national) and teamwork. This more complex model is at play in most international and global teams.

Level III also requires an understanding of one's own leadership style and the impact we create in the team. The Level III approach is most in-depth and it helps to inject the right energy and motivation into the team, and to lead the team in a fluid and adaptable way by providing strong focus and emotional stability whilst taking account of changing external environments and volatility and adapting over time.

Level I: Governance – Basic Frameworks

There are many frameworks to improve team performance but one that has been consistently influential was developed by Katzenbach and Smith in *The Wisdom of Teams* (1993). This model was further developed by Katzenbach Partners, providing a definition of the team that is extremely useful as a checklist of key criteria. It allows us to diagnose whether we are dealing with a working group, a pseudo-team, a real team or a high-performance team.

Table 2.1 Main differences between working groups and teams (following Katzenbach and Smith, 1993)

Working group	Team
• individual accountability	• individual and collective accountability
• individual goals and outputs	• collective goals and outputs
• focus on efficient meetings	• focus on real discussion and collective problem-solving

According to Katzenbach and Smith (1993), a team is "a small number of people with complementary skills, who are committed to a common purpose, set of performance goals and approach for which they hold themselves mutually accountable", indicating all the checklist questions for good governance in a team:

▷ A common purpose and commitment
▷ Performance goals
▷ Mutual accountability
▷ Complementary skills.

A working group is a collection of individuals who report to each other, with individual goals but no collective goals. Table 2.1 shows the main differences between working groups and teams.

These few differentiators already show one of the key features of effective teams – discussion, engagement and collective problem-solving. How many teams that you know have a *real* dialogue and approach business problems in a creative way? Isn't the need for effective dialogue particularly pressing in the current economic uncertainty?

Many teams do not reach the basic ("101") level of good governance but are stuck at the level of pseudo-teams, where there is a clear need for a common output but the team either does not subscribe to it, engages in in-fighting and is competitive within, or has a team leader who has not introduced the basic steps to achieve good governance.

The basic recommendations of this model include:

▷ Define clear team goals
▷ Give focus and direction

▷ Set a few immediate performance-oriented tasks and goals – apart from the longer term strategic aims
▷ Select team members on the basis of skills and potential, not personality. This may be a reaction against Belbin's team types, which are more personality based, as we saw in Chapter 1
▷ Define clear rules of behavior and expectations
▷ Challenge the group regularly against complacency
▷ Use positive feedback, recognition and reward to create and sustain positive dynamics and the momentum to create team performance (Chapter 4 shows a case study for introducing team governance).

In their original article on teams, the authors also comment that teams at the top are "certainly the most difficult...and that real teams at the top were often smaller and less formalized.... They were mostly twos or threes, with an occasional fourth" (Katzenbach & Smith, 1993a, p.171). As we know, at the top of companies, we often find a core team or a trio of CEO, COO and CFO, and an extended executive management team of 8 to 12 executives.

Katzenbach and Smith's model provides an excellent basic governance or "hygiene" framework. Any team will benefit from looking at its core components. The model also gives a definition of high-performance teams: beyond the components of the original definition, you need team members "who are deeply committed to one another's personal growth and success" (Katzenbach & Smith, 1993, p.92), a team that has the dynamics that seem intangible and cannot be planned and organized, yet be facilitated by an effective leadership style. The way to get here is not really further explained by Katzenbach and Smith but the Level III approach will outline ideas to develop high-performing global teams.

How can we get the right skill sets and what issues should we consider to understand the skill set of the team, its strengths, weaknesses and gaps?

Level II: Skills – The Competencies

▷ A recent meeting with a large private equity firm illustrates the challenge of finding the right talent at the top. Despite the global success of the business, populated with smart, internationally educated executives, the company admitted to having problems identifying and appointing the right people at the top, not just chief executives but any crucial roles at the executive level. This firm, like many private equity firms, is looking for a more sophisticated approach to assess senior talent as well as a way of educating the operating partners to become more astute assessors of "human capital".

▷ CEO selections and CEO failures are in the limelight and have sparked an intense focus of most boards on succession management. How could the board of Hewlett-Packard (and many other boards for that matter) have got it so wrong and ended up churning four CEOs in two and a half years, leading *Business Week* to publish an article with the question Can HP Innovate?, and answering "yes" with regard to talent drain (11 January 2013). The board probably went through a perfectly viable selection process, assisted by third parties and taking the necessary deliberation before making any of the appointments that subsequently failed. So how can the selection and succession be improved? After nearly two decades in the search industry, my view is the following: although processes have been improved, search needs to get much better at advising corporations and incorporate the best of business school research in doing so – not an easy gap to bridge but achievable.

Looking at business school research, there is a very interesting approach that gives practical recommendations for succession management of chief executives. In 2001, Rakesh Khurana, then an Assistant Professor at Harvard Business School, published an excellent and very practical article "Finding the right CEO: Why Boards Often Make Poor Choices". Khurana researched the board processes of large US corporations in selecting their chief executives. His research was based in the period of 1995 to 2000 and his conclusion that "because of entrenched but rarely questioned" practices, boards often failed to choose the right chief executives, suggests that not much has changed more than a decade later. Based on an examination of 100 CEO successions and on the basis of interviews with board directors, executive search consultants and chief executive candidates, he identified a series of pitfalls that boards and selection teams continuously make and that need to be addressed to ensure more success in getting it right:

1. **Most boards do not engage in the necessary analysis or organizational introspection that will lead to success.**
   In CEO transitions, the pressure by investors and financial institutions, as well as media, to close the leadership gap leads to the preference of "speed over fit". Often there is a lack of clarity regarding criteria for success, as many "boards rushed to identify candidates before pausing to re-evaluate goals" (Khurana, 2001, p.92). Nomination and search committees often draw up a list of ideal candidate attributes that read like superman or superwoman's description, rather than first specifying the strategic goals and strategic demands of the role over time and then working backwards to decide on the criteria – ultimately engaging in a search with more clarity. I have always advocated the need to select on the basis of strategy (Marx, 2001, 2002, 2011) – this will do two things: first, it expands the pool of potential candidates as otherwise we typically search too narrowly; second, it reduces the risk of comparing candidates in terms of personalities rather than in terms of future needs of the organization. This results in more objective decision-making and minimizes the human pitfall we all have: recruiting in our own image.
2. **Having the wrong search committees.**
   According to Khurana, search committees need to be deeply familiar with the company and its history (i.e. having at least some long-tenured board member on the nominations committee) and to have some diversity of background – an aspect that is expanded on in Chapter 6.
3. **Simply equating CEO candidates with the performance of their past companies.**
   "In almost every CEO search studied, the performance of candidates' current company was weighed without regard to the candidate's influence on it" (Khurana, 2001, p.95).

It is a damning conclusion after analyzing 100 CEO successions of US boards; and we are likely to find similar results all over the world. In my experience with European companies, for example, the work and process of the nomination committee is least understood (as opposed to the audit or remuneration committees). The practical guidelines that Khurana suggested in 2001 still hold today:

▷ Expand the composition of the search committee to include diversity
▷ Recognize that the CEO alone cannot be the panacea but analyze the composition of the top team in relation to the strategic goals
▷ Take an outcome-oriented approach: evaluate candidates against the requirements of the position rather than against each other.

How can a selection that is based on strategic goals of the organization be implemented in practice?

Strategic skills assessment

Imagine yourself on the board of directors of a large and complex company in the engineering sector, with the task of replacing the outgoing CEO as soon as possible. You have two final candidates with relatively similar business experience but very different functional backgrounds. The board does not entirely agree on the future strategic direction and needs to come up with a decision fast: is the functional background an indicator on which to base the selection decision?

Miles and Snow (1978) answered this question with an emphatic "yes" and started a series of research studies on top management teams (TMTs), later developed in to the Upper Echelon Theory (Hambrick and Mason, 1984). Miles and Snow provided a typology to measure the effect of top executives' characteristics on strategic choices and organizational performance. Essentially, they recommended that, ideally, top executives should be selected and matched to the strategic intent of the company. They divide organizations into three strategic types:

1. The *prospectors* are organizations where innovation, flexibility and new product and market development are paramount

2. The *defenders* focus on efficiency and cost reductions as their main strategies to achieve competitive advantage
3. The *analyzers* develop hybrid strategies between the prospectors and defenders. They can use both and adapt flexibly to the requirements of the external environment.

Miles and Snow (1978) assumed that prospectors have a larger proportion of outward-oriented executives. The defenders in contrast were seen as being dominated by internally focused executives, "more likely from an engineering or accounting background". Moreover, defender organizations have more senior executives promoted from within (understanding the details of the efficiency of cost-cutting drives) and executives have longer tenure.

The breakthrough idea of Miles and Snow was to match executives to strategy – an idea that is, of course, intuitively taken up by headhunters that operate at boardroom level. This theory assumes that top executives show unique characteristics that will influence their strategic choices. Hambrick and Mason (1984) pursued this idea extensively in the Upper Echelon Theory and demonstrated the linkage between executive attributes and choice of strategy (see Chapter 5).

Business school academics were the first to assert that functional background of executives influences their strategic choice and the way they will run the business. They differentiate between:

▷ *output experience*: more likely pursued by executives with marketing, research and development backgrounds, and
▷ *throughput experience*: more likely pursued by executives with finance, engineering and manufacturing backgrounds.

Whilst output and throughput may not be particularly user-friendly terms, the concept is important in reviewing how we select top executives and put management teams together. As a psychologist, I would argue that functional background influences the way we perceive business, what we focus on and the solutions we develop to tackle business challenges. Ignoring this "conditioning" seems surprising, yet we often do so. The steps for a more strategic selection will be illustrated in detail in Case 5.1.

Translating the Miles and Snow Typology into business competencies, we would expect defender organizations to be particularly strong in operational effectiveness and prospector organizations to be strong in external market orientation, innovation and the development of visionary strategies. A practical example illustrates this. In a review of top executives of a large European corporation, with businesses all over the world, the board discussed the following findings:

> The strengths of the top team, comprised of a mix of nationalities and international locations, were completely aligned with the strategy and the culture of the business – we found excellent operational effectiveness throughout the top rank, also explaining the long-term success of the business. The risks were in the lack of external market orientation, innovation, and the risk of not spotting if the strategy needed to be changed; some of the executives were not close enough to the external markets and believed little innovation was necessary in such a successful business. The Chairman's main question recognized the risk – "Do we need new blood over time?" He realized that the group was very homogenous and was questioning whether a different input was needed.

In practice, and on the background of previous research studies, succession should be looked at in the context of the overall top team, the culture and the strategy of the company. Defender organizations (where we traditionally find long tenure and internal promotions) often need to inject new ideas as provided by externally recruited executives from different sectors and functional backgrounds.

Professor Andrew Campbell, Director of the Ashridge Strategic Management Centre (UK), who has worked extensively on this topic, has always criticized what he calls the neglect of strategy in CEO selection (personal conversation with Andrew Campbell), and he recommends focusing on "Value Proposition Assessments" to increase the success in CEO selection – and, one could argue, in any selection at executive level. To create a better candidate match, the search brief needs to include a value and strategy definition by the organization. This will allow the searcher to ascertain the candidates' ability to create value and the risk areas of value destruction.

In Campbell's view, chief executive candidates should be asked to talk about their leadership philosophy and beliefs; these are questions that are still not often asked by nomination committees and yet they allow a real insight into leaders and their values as well as their likely approach to changing business scenarios. Most of the recruitment process is often one-dimensional, focusing on technical skills.

When I asked Jacqueline Novogratz, the founder of Acumen Fund, a not-for-profit international organization based in New York, how she ensures getting the right people into an expanding international not-for-profit organization that is focused on social enterprises in the developing world (covering Africa, Asia and Latin America), she explained the dilemma succinctly: "We have learned a lot from past experience. The corporate world is typically caught up with technical skills – the not-for-profit world is caught up with passion." She sees the need to incorporate the two. "Hence we are looking for the following:

1. The right technical skill set
2. Moral imagination (i.e. empathy)
3. Being part of something that is bigger than you."

In many ways, we can apply these questions straight to the corporate sector and ask executive candidates the following questions:

1. Does the person know how to create value in the situation they are recruited for or promoted to?
2. How will the person create value? What are their leadership characteristics, drive, motivation and energy as well as hard competencies?
3. What is his or her fit with the organizational culture and the top team?

Asking these three questions will reduce the number of cases where previously successful executives do not perform in a new organization. We need a more sophisticated analysis and prediction as to how the CEO and the executive team as a whole will influence the strategy and performance of the company through more targeted assessments (see Chapter 5 for case examples and methodologies). This type of assessment will also help us to understand two types of CEOs: the constantly successful CEOs who are able to develop and implement defender and prospector strategies, i.e. the adapters; and those CEOs whose performance dips in the case of strategic changes and who do not adapt easily.

Cultural differences in functional backgrounds of CEOs

From a search perspective, in the UK CEOs often have accountancy and finance backgrounds, German CEOs often have engineering or law backgrounds, and American chief executives are likely to arrive with an advanced degree and an MBA in the boardroom.

My own research on transatlantic comparisons between British and US CEOs showed the following results: 34 percent of CEOs of British companies had an accounting/finance background compared to 26 percent of CEOs of the Fortune 100 US companies. Furthermore, the percentage of accountants amongst British CEOs has increased to 50 percent in CEOs appointed after the onset of the economic crisis (Marx, 2008, 2011), probably a direct effect of the crisis as boards want more directors with strong financial backgrounds. The career backgrounds of the CEOs of a country's largest companies are a role model for aspiring executives at any level, as they provide objective indicators on how to get to the top. The cross-cultural differences of CEO career patterns also show us what is valued in a particular country/business culture. Can we simply equate output experience with external orientation and throughput experience with internal orientation?

Are companies with a strong presentation of marketing and research & development in the top team better at adapting to external markets, in terms of business development and innovation, and companies with stronger finance, engineering and manufacturing expertise better at creating efficiencies and ensuring a strong balance sheet?

The current crisis in the UK, with its over-reliance on financial services and a decaying manufacturing sector, has put politicians on the alert, with a long overdue drive to increase the number of science and engineering graduates and focus on research & development.

The match between executive characteristics and strategy

Does this match improve business performance? In a study of Fortune 500 US firms, Thomas and Ramaswamy (1996) demonstrated that the match between executive characteristics and strategy had a positive effect on organizational performance. These researchers also showed that *prospector* executives were significantly younger, had higher levels of education and shorter tenures than their *defender* counterparts. As the authors comment, "the findings show the need for a more comprehensive framework that incorporates executives' attributes, strategy, and organizational performance" and "the results...could enhance the effectiveness of managerial selection and recruitment" (p.258). Can the use of simple demographic data enhance the success of executives at the top of companies? Most companies have a mix of executives and often a mix of strategies. Depending on the exact business phase, the company may pursue a *prospector* strategy of innovation when markets are buoyant and *defender* strategy in recessionary times – ultimately, the *analyzer* is the really adaptive organization of the future. This again supports the need for agility and diversity at the top and points to an indepth understanding of this diversity in terms of leadership skills of the chief executive to manage and use the diversity effectively.

One can also argue that expecting the match between executives' attributes and strategy to automatically produce results is simplistic. As Professor Andrew Pettigrew of Oxford's Saïd Business School has repeatedly argued, one needs to understand and analyze the intervening processes: top management teams have dynamics and operate in a highly complex and changing business environment. A static model such as the original Miles and Snow model cannot account for this complexity. Hambrick and Mason (1984) introduced a model that takes account of some of the intervening processes that may take place in the form of personality characteristics, values and leadership style of the chief executive. They try to fill the "black box" (Lawrence, 1997) between the demographics of the team and the subsequent strategy. These authors propose that executives' characteristics or background influence the perception or "field of vision" of business, and that an executive's perception of the business situation (combined with their values) is the basis of strategic choice.

This model draws in the psychology of the individual and the psychology of the team in understanding how a business challenge is interpreted and dealt with – the types of solution that are considered, selected and implemented. The dynamics of the team, its interactions, power-play and dramas, are often ignored – yet, as Pettigrew states, these intangibles need to be understood. To develop effective top teams, we need to understand the intangibles (Andrew Pettigrew, personal communication, 2013).

Since 2008, many boards have started to look at executive teams more critically. As one chairman remarked:

> ...after nearly 15 years of continuous growth, the first thing we noted with the economic crisis was that we did not have enough people with turnaround experience in the company – everyone has been "spoiled" in this ongoing growth phase. We do not have sufficient crisis experience in our executive group. What is most surprising was that our predictions of which executives would be good in a crisis did not hold up. Those who were expected to adapt and perform well often failed and could not handle it, and those we did not consider previously as star performers seem to have come through the crisis and managed the challenges very well.

This chairman's observations raise several questions:

▷ Does our "usual" prediction of executive performance still work in the current crisis and will it work in future, assuming we will have greater unpredictability and volatility?
▷ Is the neatly packaged typology of defenders and prospectors long superseded by the need for more analyzers or completely different categories?
▷ Is the analyzer organization the model of the new "*ambidextrous*" firm, incorporating output and throughput executives in a seamless way?
▷ Is the need for the analyzer organization the most convincing argument for diversity of the team which can adapt to seemingly incompatible and paradoxical challenges in today's business? Hambrick's theories have sparked a series of studies analyzing these characteristics and some of these are further reviewed in Chapter 5 and 6.

In today's business, succession management is one of the key responsibilities of company boards. Many organizations have introduced more sophisticated leadership assessments to ascertain whether the company has the right business competencies at the top. These evaluations, often carried out by search consultants, allow a sophisticated diagnosis of skills and help identify the strengths and gaps in relation to the company's strategic goals. The quantification of business skills and competencies of the executive teams is to be applauded. Yet the exclusive reliance on skill set to predict a team's performance is naïve. The top team may have all the necessary business skills but be unable to implement the skills because it may lack drive, have a leader who cannot create a vision or unite a team, or have an organizational culture that is incongruent with the strategic goals.

Staying with the CEO selection, it is often argued that the success of a business leader is 30 percent technical business skills, 30 percent personality characteristics (such as leadership style, motivation) and 40 percent match with the culture of the organization. When previously successful chief executives fail in a new company, it is often due to a lack of fit with the culture. Extending this, we may need a team model that takes these factors into account, and that is more sophisticated and goes beyond demographics and business skills.

The Level I approach to team development brings discipline, the Level II approach ensures we have the necessary business skills, and only the Level III approach will enable us to produce results in complex and changing environments by including an understanding of the psychology of the team in the context of the specific culture and strategy of the organization. Nevertheless, all three levels deserve attention as each may provide the right approach, depending on the key challenge of the team at the time and the focus of its business leader.

Every leader who manages a team, irrespective of the level, should have a Level I type team framework in place. If there is a strategic shift or new team or CEO, Level II development is indicated. But if we want to be successful in the international arena or shift the culture of an organization, a Level III approach is necessary, as it addresses the interplay between skills, psychology, strategy and culture.

Level III: Dynamics – Global Team Development

The dynamics and interplay of teams are particularly noticeable in global teams: how do global teams leverage their cultural diversity? Do organizations have frameworks for developing global teams that cover global markets? The following case examples illustrate how organizations in very different sectors, from philanthropic to financial institutions, approach the development of global teams.

> **Case Example 2.1: Global Teams at the Rockefeller Foundation**
>
> The Rockefeller Foundation was formed in 1913 and opened its first overseas office in 1914 in Bangkok. "One could say that since that time, Rockefeller employees have been working as global teams," observes Samantha Gilbert, the Chief Human Resources Officer of the Rockefeller Foundation. "We have an archive which documents the international progress very well. There are letters from the Bangkok office to their colleagues in New York, reporting on their findings, developments and specific needs in Asia, and their New York colleagues responding to them" – examples of international team collaboration in 1914.
> When asked about the Rockefeller Foundation's framework or model for international teams, Samantha Gilbert commented:
>
> We have guiding principles rather than prescriptive frameworks on how to put a team together. These consist of:
>
> ▷ The importance of regular communication
> ▷ The effective use of technology
> ▷ Sharing the burden of time differences throughout the business
> ▷ Specific training and development for individual members and teams, including some coaching
> ▷ Pointers on how to work when people have dotted-line reporting around the world.
>
> To ensure effective international teams, Samantha Gilbert, who previously worked in a commercial organization, started to

introduce some of the best practices from the for-profit sector into this philanthropic organization.

One of the major differences in organizational development that I found between the profit and not-for-profit sectors was the use of some successful people-development tools, such as performance coaching. This development tool was fairly new in the philanthropic sector when I introduced it to the Foundation. Although there was slight resistance initially, coaching has been received in a very positive way, once the absolute confidentiality of this intervention was clearly communicated and understood. Coaching has now been successful for five years at our Foundation. It has been particularly effective in helping individuals to bring management and leadership skills to a higher level. For example, if you are a manager in Karachi and have team members in Nairobi, Jakarta and other locations, you need to make sure to delegate the work evenly and effectively. There is often the temptation to give the most interesting work to people in your own office – which does not generate a well-functioning global team. Coaching managers for skills development, especially in a global context, has positive dividends toward creating high-performing teams.

We also focus on team retreats to help the bonding of the team. In a philanthropic organization, the alignment of values of the individual and the team with the organizational goals is paramount. One of the key values, and this is reflected in our selection criteria, is a deep appreciation of the value of diversity. This is best demonstrated through an investment of learning-time together. Apart from the social and emotional bonding, team retreats are essential for effective discussion of the strategy, to hear and apply different perspectives to strategy development to ensure it more robustly reflects the needs of the work. In order to guarantee an external and objective view, and to move the team forward toward embracing and appreciating differences as we formulate strategy, we also often work with facilitators in our team retreats.

Do teams in a philanthropic organization have less stress compared to global teams in a commercial organization?

Stress is probably universal across all sectors: the work here is demanding, coupled with time differences. For teams in Asia, for example, holding conference calls with New York at the end of their busy day, plus the travel component of the Foundation, can easily add up to very stressful work demands. Although the Rockefeller Foundation has not in recent years experienced

2 ▶ TEAM EFFECTIVENESS

> the burden of downsizing, work/life balance is a big issue and we need to be constantly aware of that. An organization with 100 years of international experience addressing fundamental global issues, such as poverty, and an organization that looks at the long-term impact addressing global issues (while making sure the specific interventions and projects work at the local level) reflects the challenges of international teams.
>
> The selection criteria for international team members at the Rockefeller Foundation illustrate a highly differentiated approach. Samantha Gilbert lists the following as key criteria in selection:
>
> ▷ People who thrive in international environments
> ▷ Passion for the type of work
> ▷ People who love the dynamics of international work on teams and the complexity of it. This enjoyment and stimulation often makes up for the long hours
> ▷ People who have demonstrated the ability to adapt to changing environments
> ▷ A deep appreciation of the value of diversity
> ▷ High threshold for ambiguity as things are unclear
> ▷ Patience. Things take longer in a global context
> ▷ Strong active listening skills, particularly important in the team leaders.
>
> We look at predominately soft criteria when building internationally effective team members.

This is even reflected in the fundamental shift of the "hard-nosed" financial services sector.

> ### Case Example 2.2: Global Teams in Financial Services
>
> The Chairman of Citi Asia, Shirish Apte, an Indian-born executive with a long-standing career at Citi and senior responsibilities in different parts of the world, describes here the changes in and key challenges for international teams in financial services:
>
> > There has been a clear change in the financial services industry over the last 15 to 20 years, and this change is particularly evident

in the emerging markets. In the seventies and eighties, banking in the emerging markets was relatively basic. Besides, domestic financial institutions had limited ability for raising large amounts of capital, including debt, equity and loans, from domestic markets and corporations had to rely on external markets for financing large projects. As a result, capital markets expertise for both debt and equity was principally focused in developed markets, which was where the providers of this capital resided. Most international banks therefore followed a hub-and-spoke structure for global teams with major financial centres such as London, New York, Tokyo, etc. being the hubs for sophisticated product expertise and access to international investors. These teams were in turn supported by local coverage teams. Global teams would fly in from hubs (sometimes known as "suitcase bankers") as needed and their global calling card became a selling point with corporations in the emerging markets. Thus local bankers became "order takers" rather than true partners in this relationship. Twenty years on, things have changed. Many large emerging economies have well-developed and well-capitalized financial institutions, many of them in the private sector, with the ability to support large-scale financing. Many of the domestic markets also provide sophisticated capital market products, and there are increasing flows among emerging economy countries rather than just the developed-to-emerging flows of the past. Clearly, these changes are reflected in the composition of global teams. While there are still hubs of expertise structured by product and industry, the local coverage teams are much stronger. Besides, some of these hubs are now located in large emerging economies depending on location of capital, and business opportunity.

These developments and changes have also impacted the way global financial institutions hire and train people. Whereas in the past a cadre of international bankers would be moved around to hubs, today many of these bankers live in their home countries and call on experts as necessary. In many instances, on-ground relationship with key clients has become very critical. This has given rise to a group of domestic bankers with broad product expertise who can call upon appropriate resources in their organization while being seen as advisors to their clients. Most importantly, the focus is on a broad multicultural ability of bankers, as global financial institutions take a relationship and culture-based approach.

How have the selection criteria for recruitment changed over the last 15 years?

While the basic training remains the same, there is much greater emphasis on a well-rounded experience. In the past, bankers would view a move to a developed market hub as an end in itself. Today this is viewed as a transition point with an understanding that the future for the banker could well be back in the home country as a senior coverage or product banker.

The key criteria nowadays are:

▷ Multicultural experience
▷ The ability to work in different environments
▷ The ability to work in "flexible teams" [project teams].

There is another important change in financial services that is driving the composition of global teams, and that change is the commoditization of financial products. In the past, certain financial institutions had a special area of expertise in either equities or debt capital markets, for example, or in specific industries. These areas of differentiation have largely disappeared and most global financial institutions have broadly similar capability to structure and execute large sophisticated transactions across most markets. As a result, financial institutions are shifting from a product-focused to a client-centric coverage model. At the same time, the coverage model itself is changing. Over the last 15 years, global markets have converged. Energy, metals and mining, telecoms have become global industries requiring, in many cases, global coverage. In such an environment, global financial institutions need global coverage teams with cross-functional expertise, including high-end capital markets products together with transaction services capabilities supporting global industries. Over time, the financial services industry has changed from domestic banking to product-focused coverage, and now to a multi-dimensional product- and industry-focused client-centric model.

The product silos of the past are changing to flexible teams and this requires a mindset shift. This new environment has also changed leadership requirements: the need is for team champions, not bosses, who are able to lead multicultural, multi-product teams and who have a much deeper understanding of their clients. The team leader derives his/her authority not anymore from the title the person carries, but from the team realizing that this person can get things done with the client and with their own organization.

What are the specific challenges to make this work?

A key element of the success of the new structure is to ensure that every one on the team understands their role and feels a part of the overall result. There is always a risk of teams becoming

> too large and creating confusion with the client. Besides, from a client point of view, one person has to have accountability for delivering results, so this person, generally the team leader, must have the credibility and authority among the team to make decisions. The other issue is deal size and flexibility. Large multi-discipline teams, at times, have differing goals from local coverage players. Clients expect their advisors to cover a multitude of transactions for them, big and small with varying degrees of profitability. This often does not fit with the objectives of the global bankers. It becomes the responsibility of the team leader to resolve these differences and again the credibility of the team leader helps drive this process.

Shirish Apte, with his long-standing banking career in various parts of the world, describes the shift in financial services as:

▷ From simple solutions to complex services
▷ From transactions to long-term client relationships
▷ From global business centre domination to a mix of local and international teams
▷ Most importantly, a shift from the individualistic banker or star trader to someone who can lead or work in these international, flexible teams, and changing the often short-term oriented to longer term perspectives.

In essence, a shift of mindset.

Spending money on team development is often seen as a good thing to do but with uncertain effects – the kind of activity you do when the economy is performing well. Whilst everyone will agree that a truly effective and cohesive team is a positive thing, it is often difficult to quantify what difference it makes to the bottom line or to find the right approaches to get there, producing hard financial results. As a consequence, too many companies still tend to see systematic development of the top team as maybe nice to do but lacking in rigor, an optional extra. The basic question is whether the value of any team development can be quantified, i.e. what is the evidence in producing results? Looking at different approaches to team development, many frameworks are "lopsided"; they either focus on the psychological arena or look primarily at strategy development.

The Link-up Between Psychology, Cultural Context and Strategy

An effective approach to developing global teams is to provide a link-up between the psychology of the team, the cultural context and the strategic goals of the business. This link-up between psychology–context–strategy produces real business results, as demonstrated in Case 3.1, where a team intervention based on this model produced a revenue increase of over 60 percent. Demonstrating "hard" data (financial results) is the only way to convince business leaders to engage in more systematic development of their top teams.

The psychology–context–strategy model uses the clarification of the psychological make-up and the context/culture, whether organizational or national, the team operates in as a platform to implement the business strategy. What will become clear in this approach is that unless a team manages its own diversity and differences effectively, it is unlikely to manage the diversity of its clients and the markets it is operating in. The era of pretty predictable business scenarios is probably over and we need business teams that are agile not only in recognizing this but in responding to it – by applying more sophisticated approaches that leave room for continuous adaptation.

This requires a certain level of self-understanding. Unless a CEO and the top team have an understanding of their own skill sets, their psychological make-up and the cultural context in which they are operating, the implementation of strategy is left to chance.

Looking at the issue of diversity, as a first step a psychological approach makes the diversity of the team transparent and overt, both in its positive and potentially negative ways. In fact, the key challenge of global teams is to understand and manage its own diversity. It then allows the team to use its diversity positively in generating better business solutions and in understanding its clients better, while counteracting the negative effects of diversity, such as emotional tensions, "charged" disagreements and rows in the team.

In summary, the psychological model of global teams allows transparency in the team, the pinpointing of its strengths and

Table 2.2 The key components of the psychology–context–strategy approach to global teams

Psychological Components	Context	Strategy
The psychological profile of the team • How global is the team? • Where does it sit on the Culture Shock Triangle? *Cognitive skills* • Understanding of global issues and capacity to produce effective solutions *Behavioral aspects* • Effective communication and transnational social skills • Networking skills *Emotional aspects* • Confidence and stress management • Ability to deal with risk and ambiguity • Self-management of emotions	*The national cultures the teams and its clients operate in* • What is the effect of the business culture? • Divisional subcultures or functional subcultures	*Strategic goals* • Global growth • Restructuring • Changing the organization to a more performance-oriented one and implementing organizational change

problem areas and how it interacts with the outside world. The approach requires some level of analysis but is then extremely action-oriented and practical.

The key components of the psychology–context–strategy alignment are described in Table 2.2.

The case studies in this book will look at these components in detail and show how to incorporate them in practice.

Culture Shock in Teams

Global teams need to adapt to cultural differences and complexities in their everyday work, whether they are setting up emerging market operations in South America or Eastern Europe, dealing with international customers from their home base or taking a strategic view on how to expand their international footprint. They also need to deal with their own cultural differences day to day.

In my earlier writing, I have argued that international executives need to manage the "culture shock" of doing business abroad. Culture shock is the experience of foreignness which occurs when expectations and reality do not coincide. The same happens in international teams: the clashing of different views about the world, the business and the way to achieve results.

Dealing with international team diversity is essentially dealing with culture shock. The term "culture shock" was originally introduced by the anthropologist Oberg (1960) and he identified several indicators:

▷ Anxiety and anger
▷ Confusion about roles and values
▷ Strain
▷ Feelings of helplessness
▷ Sense of loss for those who expatriate.

While international teams may not typically experience the same depth and extent of culture shock symptoms typically associated with expatriation, many of us have been in international teams where emotions are flying high and frustration and irritability are expressed to a great extent. Sometimes this leads to a stalling of any further collaboration; "culture" in these instances is then used as an excuse for team failure. But often, the emotional rupture and heavy disagreements are seen as signs of positive, cognitive diversity and the team leader is able to manage the emotions and to move the team to the next stage of developing new and more effective solutions as a result. Just as Oberg saw the experience of culture shock in expatriates as necessary for effective adaptation to a foreign country, one could argue that the symptoms of culture clashes in international teams are the stepping stones to develop more effective and innovative collaborations.

Managing the three areas of the Culture Shock Triangle

The emotional side

The resilience level of the team and its leader will to some extent determine how diversity will play out; as argued in Chapter 1, we need emotionally resilient leaders who can hold the tension in the team that arises from different views of the world and from the different ways in which these views are expressed. As we will see in Chapter 6, which explores Board Diversity, the difference in perspectives of diverse teams, the cognitive diversity, will only lead to innovative and more effective problem-solving if the affective element of diversity is managed. And this depends on the self-management skills of the leader and, over time, the emotional management of the team. Similarly, one should look how the team deals with threats, negative information and risk. Does it assess risk productively or simply ignore risk and pretend that signs of impending threats are irrelevant? Or is it inclined to see most actions as risky and become paralysed? The recent massive banking crisis, which was caused by a systemic failure to perceive and handle risk effectively, should certainly prompt global teams to discuss this issue more overtly. This is not simply resolved by setting up more risk-management committees but by introducing a different attitude and dialogue on risk factors at most levels. As we will see later, the emotional make-up of the team significantly influences its thinking and problem-solving processes.

The thinking side

The mind shift in financial services that Shirish Apte earlier alluded to is a shift that is probably necessary in many sectors where flexible project teams are operating, for example, consultancies, IT companies or engineering services, where global customer orientation requires an understanding of more wide-ranging customer needs. International work requires us to do something that is inherently uncomfortable: question ourselves, question the way we are operating, and challenge some of our most fundamental approaches and values of what is right and wrong. Dogmatism, digging in one's heels and lack of questioning lead to a failure in business deals or in safeguarding the success of mergers. We often need to turn our notions on their head and have a cognitive shake-up in order to achieve more flexibility in seeing the world differently and expand our way of thinking, both of which are necessary to be a global executive.

The clever advertisements promoting HSBC as the "global bank for local organizations" probably show this best: the same image has different meanings and elicits different emotional reactions depending on the cultural angle we are taking or the culture we are coming from. HSBC's "points of value" advertising campaign is thought provoking because it shows how different cultures interpret the same image in totally different ways depending on their cultural points of view. The advertisements, often displayed in airports on the gangway to the plane, are perfect "cultural conditioners" to prepare every executive boarding the plane to regard forthcoming business negotiations in a broader way and to integrate diverse, and often contradictory, interpretations. It also hints at the necessity of suspending judgement. With this advertising campaign, HSBC has branded itself as the worldwide local bank taking pride in its understanding of cultural differences. Most importantly, this excellent advertising campaign and external branding (HSBC is ranked the Number One financial services brand by Brand Finance, with a value of $27.1 billion) is mirrored internally by a long-standing history in developing global leaders. HSBC has an established history of identifying and developing globally effective leaders in its international cadre. This cadre, originally consisting of several hundred executives, was internationally mobile, signed up for life-long careers at HSBC, would be moved to run country operations in different parts of the world and sent as global troubleshooters to sort out emergency scenarios.

Essentially, the members of the international cadre were identified early on as high-fliers. They also originally had the condition of single status attached to the start of their training in Hong Kong. One senior executive of the bank recounted how he had to present his fiancée to his boss to get his boss's approval as to the fiancée's international adaptability and mobility. Whilst this requirement has of course changed, the focus on global leadership competencies is still highly prevalent at HSBC, including the core criteria of respecting and understanding cultural differences.

How can we understand business cultures better?

Hofstede (1994) and Trompenaars (1993) have provided us with excellent research and frameworks of cultural differences, including empirical data on where a particular country is on different dimensions. Their models provide a very useful background reference and understanding of potential cultural differences. In day-to-day business situations, however, we rarely have the luxury of going through seven dimensions, as originally proposed by Trompenaars. Rather we may prefer a more practical model that prompts us to think about potential cultural differences in many business scenarios. From my experience with global leaders and their teams, and incorporating some of the research dimensions, I have developed a pragmatic approach which, similar to the HSBC advertisements, forces us to "shake up" our entrenched cultural notions by asking three simple questions:

1. Is the focus in this business culture primarily on the task at hand or on people?
2. Are frameworks here more important than flexibility?
3. What is the dominant communication style? Is a neutral style preferred or an emotionally expressive one?

1. **Task versus people orientation**
   Cultures differ as to what they value in business, whether they primarily focus on the short-term "task at hand" or the relationship between people. This mirrors the differentiation between individualistic and collectivistic cultures. Highly individualistic and task-oriented cultures are the USA or the UK, i.e. the Anglo-Saxon model, and some Northern European cultures. Of course, this stereotypes cultures and there may be businesses in the US and the UK that have a combination of the two values. Also, as a Singaporean executive recently remarked, "the old distinction between Western individualism and Asian collectivism is probably a little too simplistic". However, the short-term financial orientation of most Anglo-Saxon businesses supports the view that many companies value the immediate objectives and financial results very highly. Organizationally, this means that individual executives typically have autonomy, are individually rewarded and can make certain business decisions without referring back to headquarters. Speed is the essence here.

Collectivistic societies, as Hofstede or Trompenaars describe, are the societies with a focus on communitarianism; the group takes precedence, implying no individual executive makes decisions without referring back to the group, and often individual performance rewards do not work. Autonomy is not expected and often employees expect clear instruction. Collectivistic societies, as in traditional China, also tend to focus on building relationships first and on the business objectives later on. In these business cultures, one tries to get to know international counterparts better socially before engaging in a project or negotiations. The impatient, fast and task-oriented "type A" executive is, therefore, not very effective in cultures that put more focus on the relationship side of business and that require an orientation of achieving "tasks through people".

2. **Frameworks versus flexibility**
Some cultures work with tight schedules and frameworks – these are also cultures where predictability is valued and reliability in all matters is seen as an important attribute of good business. Typical of this approach is the German business culture – companies in Germany commonly have strong processes, and high-quality training, explaining why Germany is so strong in engineering and technology. Products work well and are well designed and thought through. But what are the drawbacks? "Lack of flexibility and dogmatic attitudes" some critics argue, especially business partners who come from the opposite side of the spectrum, from cultures that value flexibility rather than sticking to the prearranged process. French businesses, for example, often have a much more fluid approach; they are not too preoccupied with agendas and, therefore, can change direction quite quickly. The Airbus collaboration between France and Germany has produced some persistent and well-publicized tensions due to these business differences.

The difference between the importance of frameworks versus flexibility is also related to tolerance of ambiguity. "Framework-obsessed" cultures often do not like ambiguity and have a low tolerance of it. Cultures with high flexibility typically juggle different activities at the same time; they can change and refocus as they are more fluid. Framework-obsessed cultures are less fluid and prefer sequential management of their time, i.e. they go from A to B to C whereas non-sequential cultures go from A to C then back to B.

However, in complex situations, objectives are not achieved in a straight line, as John Kay, the highly regarded economist, describes in *Obliquity*. Obliquity is the principle that complex goals are best achieved indirectly. As Kay explains, "obliquity is necessary because we live in a world of uncertainty and complexity; the problems we encounter aren't always clear – and we often can't pinpoint what our goals are anyway; circumstances change; people change – and are infuriatingly hard to predict" (Kay, 2011). This sounds very much like international business to me. Kay makes a convincing case for obliquity in a diversity of challenges: from the "routes to happiness" that reward those who do not focus on it but follow indirect ways to happiness, to companies that make shareholder returns their Number One goal but, as Kay shows, these most profit-oriented companies aren't usually the most profitable ones.

With increasing business complexity, interconnectedness and globalization, the case for obliquity seems stronger than ever! People who do well in expatriate assignments and international work are those who can deal with ambiguity, who do not revert to "black and white" solutions and adapt flexibly to the "grey" situations they encounter. This is not just a cultural dimension but also a matter of individual personality, particularly one's emotional make-up and cognitive style, as we will see in the next chapter.

The global business world requires an "oblique approach" by establishing basic frameworks or processes and complementing these with a real capacity to be creative, fluid and adaptive in a fast changing environment; this seems the only way to be successful in today's uncertain environment.

Maybe this is best described by Kay's assertion of the advantages of "muddling through"; sometimes it seems

surprising how British businesses, often relying on "muddling through" and not planning to a very high degree, are so successful internationally – is it because the British have a high tolerance for and confidence to manage ambiguity?
3. **Neutral versus emotional communication style**
In neutral cultures (UK, Northern Europe and China), emotional calmness and control are highly valued and business situations require a rather neutral and rational communication approach. Rational and professional presentation approaches are most prevalent and no one expects a passionate presentation will win the argument. On the opposite side of the spectrum are some of the Latin business cultures.

Anyone who has done business in Italy and South America will know how emotional some of the debates can become and that showing one's feelings is positively perceived. In contrast, in Asian countries (China or Japan), emotional expression of anger or frustration results in "loss of face" and respect. There are also large cross-cultural differences about the type of emotional expression that is acceptable. For example, as researchers Harré and Parrott (1996) have shown, the US values positive impression management; children are trained in preschool and school to talk about their achievements and to be aware of their positive attributes. Optimism and positive self-presentation are highly valued in American society. The expression of negative emotions or self-effacing behavior is often not welcome.

Social skills and identity

The new global leaders, or as Linda Brimm (2010) calls them "global cosmopolitans", may have homes in London, Delhi and San Francisco and not only conduct business or run an IT company from these centres but also build a social circle in them. This "transnational community" is mirrored in the group of CEOs of the UK's largest FTSE 100 companies. In 1996, at the start of my research, 42 percent of the 100 CEOs of these companies had international experience (defined as a minimum of one year working abroad). By 2007, this figure had increased to 67 percent. There was a further increase in international experience among chief executives appointed post-economic crisis, i.e. after 2008, with 75 percent of CEOs having an international background. A better indicator of this transnational community is the number of foreign nationals at the helm of British companies. Comparing FTSE 100 with Fortune 100 CEOs showed that whereas almost one-third of the British business elite was foreign-born, this compared with just 10 percent of the US business elite.

But what is the effect on the identity of these global leaders?

There is a transglobal class of highly successful professionals, like the French banker in London, the German entrepreneur in Hong Kong and the Indian-born IT CEO in California, who transcend national boundaries and often have more in common with one another than with their own countrymen. How does this affect their sense of identity, self-perception and values? Our identities are shaped by many factors, such as past experience, family background, nationality, career and social context. We develop a stable sense of identity through belonging to clearly defined groups and associations. What is the effect of the fluidity of working and living in different places and having vastly different social circles? On the one hand, one may argue, a much richer sense of identity (often reflected in individuals who see themselves as Europeans rather than belonging to one country). On the other hand, can this transnational identity bring a lack of certainty regarding core values, an instability at an emotional level and a social restlessness?

Social skills in global settings

Since Daniel Goleman's (1996) book on emotional intelligence, we know that intellectual and technical skills are just the start of becoming a leader – effective leaders are those who can inspire, motivate and engage others. Whereas for many years this was equated with the charismatic leader, the leader as "hero", as in Jack Welch (CEO of General Electric 1981-2001), Jim Collins' work has shown that many leaders who build organizations that are successful over long periods of time are, in fact, not at all charismatic but are analytical and introverted. The best leaders have impressive social skills, they are clearly ambidextrous and show elements of psychological androgyny. They listen well, consult effectively, understand the drivers/motivation of the individual members in their top team, and can pick up the "vibes" or the atmosphere in an organization or in the executive team. They also know when they need to dictate a solution rather than consult or when they need to be assertive and close down the discussion; they can juggle between the two styles, depending on the requirements of the situation. In summary, they have a bandwidth of interpersonal skills they can apply flexibly.

Leadership assessments consistently show that the "softer" leadership skills are often not sufficiently developed and a range of business school courses and individual coaching approaches are trying to address this gap.

Consider you are sitting in a business negotiation in Shanghai. You're making tough demands regarding your expectations on the deal you're discussing and your Chinese counterparts seem neither to object nor to show high enthusiasm (as they're coming from a neutral culture). Observing the verbal and nonverbal signals on the other side of the impressive boardroom table and the deference and respect the Chinese executives have shown in all interactions, do they agree with you and will the deal go through or are they undecided and trying to buy time? Do they have major objections but will not raise these overtly at this stage? All the interpersonal signals that we can so readily gauge in our own culture are simply not present and are replaced by confusion about how to act next.

Our normal/national social codes do not automatically work in international settings. We have to sharpen our observation and sensitivity and develop a wider palette of potential behavior or more sophisticated social skills. It is similar to learning a new language – we need to expand our behavioral vocabulary. This can start with specific "dos and don'ts" of what is acceptable in different business cultures, with the aim of developing a much deeper understanding of underlying cultural values over time. A global executive needs to be emotionally confident to deal with confounding social signals, and needs to know and be able to apply the social rules of the culture to interpret someone's behavior correctly and adapt his/her communication accordingly. There are also some surprisingly positive results of the effects of international work on one's personality. In my early research on this topic (Marx, 1996), I asked this question of a large group of international executives. They reported the following positive effects:

▷ Greater confidence
▷ Better listening
▷ More tolerance and patience with people
▷ Greater sensitivity to other cultures
▷ Better understanding of people
▷ More assertiveness and independence
▷ Greater diplomacy
▷ Higher degree of flexibility.

This list of positive attributes supports the positive effect at all levels of the global leadership model, i.e. the levels of emotion, thinking and social behavior.

3 Global Teams

Experiences of Business Leaders: Samir Brikho and Shirish Apte

Building an international business and teams in emerging markets

Developing global clients, understanding the key drivers in different markets and pulling the right teams together are daily activities in most successful businesses over all sectors, whether financial services, professional services organizations or the creative industry. How do business leaders achieve these goals and what are the main challenges for leaders and their teams?

Samir Brikho, the CEO of AMEC, comments:

> In international teams, you need to spend time and focus clarifying the expectations of each other; for example, we had a situation where executives at Head Office in the UK received many complaints about one operation elsewhere, all because they had not checked and clarified the expectations of collaboration and their respective roles.

This assumption of having the same baseline and mode of operation is often automatically made in international organizations. As Samir Brikho points out:

> We need to spend more time in international teams to clarify the level of accountability abroad and who is responsible for what exactly. You need to show effective international leadership inside and outside your organization. In business development, for example, if you do not show effective international leadership when trying to

develop a significant client abroad, you may not just lose the assignment, you may just lose the whole country. We also need to reorientate ourselves on how fast the world is changing, and change our perceptions and definitions; for example, still defining China as an "emerging market" is simply unhelpful. And achieving effective global client development and coverage clearly starts with looking at the international capability of your most senior executives, of the top 100 or 200 executives. In other words, do the top level and the next level down reflect your markets in terms of international leadership capabilities?

Samir Brikho has significant experience in international organizations and transferred the best organizational practices from previous organizations, particularly from ABB, to AMEC:

> When I joined AMEC as Chief Executive in 2006, we had 100 senior executives in the company and most of them were white, male and 55 years old. There were hardly any non-British executives. I asked the management team how they manage diversity, i.e. the diversity of markets, clients and sectors we were operating in and wanted to develop further? I was immediately keen to introduce greater diversity into the company. I am not just interested in demographics but in the diversity of thinking, as reflected in different schooling and ethnic backgrounds, for example. I have observed that in many companies in France, and there are also other countries like this, the top 50 executives are more or less all from the same Grande École; one needs to ask how they can really challenge each other, when they have been educated to develop similar mindsets. I therefore introduced a diversity agenda into AMEC, aiming for a better mix of executives, one which shifts the balance away from our Anglo-Saxon background. I have also initiated a program to make sure we have ideally native speakers on the ground wherever we operate in the world.

As part of this drive, Samir Brikho also improved international customer coverage through tailored executive development.

> An example of how one can attract and cover international customers in a much more targeted way comes from my experience at

ABB. The Sales Department at ABB was tasked with global coverage. Given the diversity of ABB's market, the sales team needed to cover 20 different languages and consistently tested its sales force in the proficiency of the languages to ensure they were able to have in-depth discussions with customers. This gap analysis led to further executive development and more specific future recruitment. Transferring the ABB model to AMEC, we want to expand into the following markets: Middle East, Latin America and Australasia. Consequently, for example in the Middle East, the first question for the HR Director is: how many people do we have in the Middle East who speak Arabic? Companies can easily get complacent about this but I believe we need to be much more alert to these issues, if we want to win against the competition.

Which AMEC clearly seems to do, since Samir Brikho implemented an impressive turnaround from 2006 onwards.

The development of teams in Asia

What are the characteristics of teams in Asia?

Shirish Apte, Chairman of Citi Asia, addressed this question.

Asian markets are generally discussed in generic terms; however, there are important differences between North Asia, South Asia and, for that matter, ASEAN, which makes this generalization inappropriate. For one thing, rates of growth and drivers of growth in these sub-regions are different, which in turn drives business dynamics. Therefore, it is not accurate to talk about generic Asian teams. China clearly dominates the region and is the focus of attention for most financial institutions in the region. Teams focused on China and Greater China are located in Hong Kong, and increasingly in Shanghai and Beijing. The size, importance and some of the special attributes of the China market are driving the need for local product specialization, and industry and business expertise in the region.

On the other hand, Singapore is emerging as the non-China hub in the region, especially with its strong linkages to ASEAN and even India. Some of the larger Asian economies already have significant domestic capital markets and this is determining how financial institutions are constructing regional teams. Importantly, while Asia has emerged as a significant regional market for financial services, the developed markets of US and Europe are still important providers of capital. As such, global teams need to combine local coverage and expertise together with regional structuring and regional and global distribution.

What are the differences between teams in Europe and Asia?

Shirish Apte comments:

> Fundamentally, as you would expect, there are a lot of similarities between the way in which large Asian corporations operate and the way in which European corporations operate. There are of course some differences, such as the greater reliance on bank financing in Asia versus Europe. One important difference between the two regions is the nature of ownership. Many Asian companies, even the very large ones, tend to be family controlled, even when they are listed on stock exchanges. By contrast, many European companies are widely held and this together with much higher levels of liquidity in the banking sector in Asia tend to lead to the higher reliance on bank financing in Asia versus higher access to capital markets in Europe. These differences do influence the composition of teams in the region, with capital-markets product expertise being dominant in Europe and bank-market expertise in Asia.

What are the key challenges in building effective global teams? What do business leaders find difficult and what issues emerge when working in global teams?

There are common themes, irrespective of sectors. Mirroring the observations of Samir Brikho from the industrial sector, Shirish Apte sees the main challenge as "the perennial struggle between a transaction-driven versus a relationship-focused approach." He continues:

> The need for multi-disciplinary teams is unquestionable. Clients are demanding product, industry and distribution expertise

across several markets, and it is simply not possible for teams to be constructed without multi-product, multi-disciplinary global capabilities. The issue is that some members of such a team will have a transaction approach to a deal, while others will focus on the long-term relationship with the client. Fortunately, in most cases there is a congruence of these different goals. However, when there is a divergence, there needs to be clear understanding among the senior product and coverage heads on how to resolve such differences. In my opinion, conflict resolution is key to creating successful global teams. As teams become bigger and more complex in the sense that many key players are located far from the client, conflict resolution becomes challenging. For large multinational clients this is often easy. Global product partners will encounter these clients in different locations so it is easy for coverage teams to get support in most situations. The challenge is with large local companies where the support from global partners may not always be as forthcoming. Conflict resolution should happen as close to the client as possible. The most senior coverage person should take responsibility for this as it sets the tone with the coverage team.

The issue of drive and motivation – how are teams motivated?

The most experienced global leaders ask psychological questions in their day-to-day work with clients and in managing their teams. I asked Shirish Apte what the key to creating effective global teams is:

> In any global team, there needs to be one set of rules for driving relationships and deal sponsorship. There should be a common measure of success. While it is true that the scorecard of the coverage team will have a different emphasis from that of the product team, the successful coming together of these two drives client revenue.
>
> There is also a question as to who is deciding on the compensation for the individual team members. To facilitate more effective global teams, structural changes are needed. Teams in financial services need to be client focused, not product focused.

And how do you select the team leader? According to Shirish Apte:

> [A team leader needs] a lot of internal and external credibility and this is one big word for a lot of characteristics which include respect, top knowledge of sector or products, excellent client relationships and interaction skills, and the ability to access the right client at the right level.

Business school research has shown an interesting pattern in global teams. Gratton and Erickson's research on international teams in 15 multinational companies (2007) suggests that the success characteristics of teams also make it difficult to achieve effective collaboration or to translate diversity into global business results.

Although teams that are large, virtual, diverse and composed of highly educated specialists are increasingly critical with challenging projects, those same four characteristics make it hard for teams to get anything done. To put it another way, the qualities required for success are the same qualities that undermine success (Gratton and Erickson, 2007, p.100).

This paradox in global teams will be seen throughout this book and the following team study is a case in point.

Key challenges in a technology team

The challenges teams experience when they come under pressure to deliver and innovate against the global competition is illustrated in the example of a global technology company that approached me to run a workshop on developing international teams, and to address some of the team's specific challenges and expand its understanding of global customers. The team had been working together for about six months and described its team effectiveness as "a good start but the collaboration could be improved." To start with, I interviewed each team member to get their views on the current state of the team, areas for improvement and general recommendations. The following comments describe the challenges they were grappling with:

- "The set-up is functionally focused and so has a tendency towards silo mentality"
- "We need a better understanding of each team member's challenges and plans: more cross-functional working"
- "There is still not enough understanding of common targets and too little personal interaction"
- "Discussions tend to be very fact based. Brainstorming is difficult as creative energies seem to be low compared to when we had a more diverse mix, for example, with more marketing people"
- "Most of the team members are engineers and so they think alike. This is a positive feature because it helps the relationships, but it is also a negative one because of the lack of diversity in thinking"
- "There is a huge amount of organizational change in the current environment. What suffers a bit now is the people side, cross-team communication and the communication with internal and external stakeholders"
- "We need to identify two or three common action points to strengthen the team leadership role. To establish a joint understanding of our role"
- "We do not spend time on non-fact-based issues, how to come up with a synchronized strategy and achieve better personal alignment, how we can communicate effectively?"

These comments illustrate the necessary congruence of levels to achieve team effectiveness: from governance and alignment, to compatibility and diversity, to "softer", non-fact-based issues, such as communication and personal touch points.

What this technology team has experienced, like the teams in Gratton and Erickson's research (2007), is the real challenge of diverse teams: how to turn divergent thinking into creative solutions and build positive team dynamics. This is the main challenge in global teams.

Case 3.1: Global Team Development in Financial Services

The following case study gives a step-by-step account of how a team can be developed to achieve significant business results (in this case a revenue increase of 60 percent) and to beat the international competition in its sector.

> **Case 3.1**
>
> A top management team of a banking division ran successful operations on a regional basis in Europe and the Americas. However, as clients were becoming more global, the team needed to mirror this and to develop a more international approach. The decision was made to integrate the European team (running out of London) and the American operation (running out of New York). The main challenges were to develop a global approach to clients and bridge the European/US divide.
>
> The business leader recognized early on that there were tensions between the two financial centres and the teams were getting more and more polarized. I was approached as the cultural expert to help the teams integrate, become "more international" and develop a unified and effective global client approach.

The team was comprised of different nationalities, and had been working together for about a year. The problems were very overt and from observing a team meeting, the lack of alignment, communication problems, tension and dysfunctionality were obvious. The team showed:

- ▷ Little discipline
- ▷ A negative tone of communication
- ▷ Disrespect and scapegoating
- ▷ Individuals overtly pushed their own agendas
- ▷ There were different expectations as to the pace of client development and execution of the business
- ▷ There was no agreement on client approach

▷ There was, in fact, little discussion nor any agreed action points at the conclusion of the meeting.

On closer examination, London saw New York as "too aggressive, pushy and directive". New York saw London as "sluggish, risk averse and defensive". Not surprisingly, this cultural friction resulted in a destructive style of communication, scapegoating and a tendency to let conflicts openly fester rather than to seek resolutions. There was not only a cultural but also a functional divide in the team, which, as with many teams in financial services, consisted of business developers and transactors, i.e. those who brought the business in and those transacting it. Tension existed between these two sub-teams: the transactors blamed the business developers for not being aggressive and fast enough in developing clients. The negative dynamics did not allow the team to develop innovative solutions for their clients; in fact they were counter-productive and business results had declined.

When I came out of the original team session, I was not sure whether it was already too late for an intervention and whether I had the right approach for this team. What assured me that my approach could work were the following factors, which I examine in any project to establish whether the team can be developed and produce better business results.

Success Factors in Global Team Development

1. **Is the leader, the CEO or Managing Director, talented, motivated and interested to develop as a leader?**
   If the business leader is not technically talented, has little curiosity or openness to develop himself or herself, I am less inclined to pursue the consulting project but will give informal advice or suggest a different approach. In the current case study, the head of the business was impressive; he was highly intelligent, technically admired for his work, a strong business developer and a long-standing successful banker. He was also ambitious to succeed further and was open to learning new things – another characteristic of leaders who are successful in a global environment.

2. **Does the team show the right skills and technical competencies to be successful?**
   There was a tick in all of the boxes of the team members in this case, as they were technically extremely good.
3. **Is there enough ambition and drive in the team to pull it together towards a common goal and against the competitors?**
   One look at this financial services team showed the extraordinary drive and ambition, unfortunately often "misdirected" presently and turned internally against its own members rather than against the external competition.
4. **What drives the team members and how can they be motivated to engage, learn and change?**
   Financial services is not known for an interest in self-analysis or psychological or "softer" issues. Most executives in financial services are clearly driven by money and are switched on by numbers. On a case-by-case basis, one therefore needs to evaluate whether complex psychological or cultural issues can be made tangible and ideally numerically explainable, and do this in a "fast way" to "catch" the short-term attention of a banker audience.
5. **Can the team be directed towards a common motivational goal?**
   In this case, the common motivational goal was easy to find: making more money. In fact, there were two common goals: increasing the revenue from global clients and moving the team up in its global ranking against the competition.
6. **Will the analysis and psychological profile of the team give tangible results that can be immediately related to the strategic goals and show the intermediary steps to implement the strategy?**
   Can we synthesize the diverse factors affecting the performance of this global team? Is the synthesis strategy focused and can it be used as the basis to develop specific tactics and action steps? Teams in financial services are switched on by numbers, consequently we need objective data of cultural or psychological differences and a clear-cut way to relate the data to strategic objectives. The Psychology–Context–Culture model makes this possible.

7. **How can cultural differences be turned into creative solutions?** Culture can be defined as "the way we are doing things" or, as Hofstede summed it up, it is the "software of the mind". Culture is the construction of a model we use to understand the world – whether this is organizational culture or national culture. Hofstede was one of the first to outline the various layers in which cultures express themselves. These include:

Symbols (greetings, dress code)
Heroes (national figures)
Rituals (ceremonies)
Values.

The business head was clearly committed and after confirming the commitment of the whole team, we decided on a two-fold approach: a combination of individual and team development.

The challenge was quite steep – to turn a group of highly individualistic, competitive bankers into a global team. Fortunately, we had clear common goals from the outset: the team wanted to be global leader in its market and make more money. To achieve this, it needed to become more international, increase the international client-deal flow and boost group intelligence. We agreed a course that included a combination of self- and team development to help each executive increase their global capability as well as addressing the team's capability. Whenever a team needs to drive major strategic changes (which globalization clearly is), a combination of self- and team development will get results as opposed to working only at group level.

A Step-by-step Approach

Table 3.1 gives an overview of the Psychology–Context–Strategy model in relation to the present case study.

To match the high results-orientation of financial services, we agreed on an action-oriented approach, a step-by-step approach of what the team needed to do to achieve its specific objectives and to make more money for the business. The project included a

Table 3.1 The challenges of the global financial services team

Psychological	Context	Strategy
• highly individualistic and competitive executives • high task-orientation • fast paced • low global effectiveness	• business culture divide (London versus New York) • national culture effect • international clients • sub-team of business developers and transactors	• being Number One in global ranking • increasing global clients-deal flow • increasing international group intelligence

EMOTIONS
- Drive and ambition
- Motivation
- Stress resistance
- Self-confidence

BEHAVIOR AND SOCIAL SKILLS
- Team orientation
- Relationship skills
- Communication
- Intro- and extraversion
- Interpersonal sensitivity
- Tolerance as to different styles of behavior

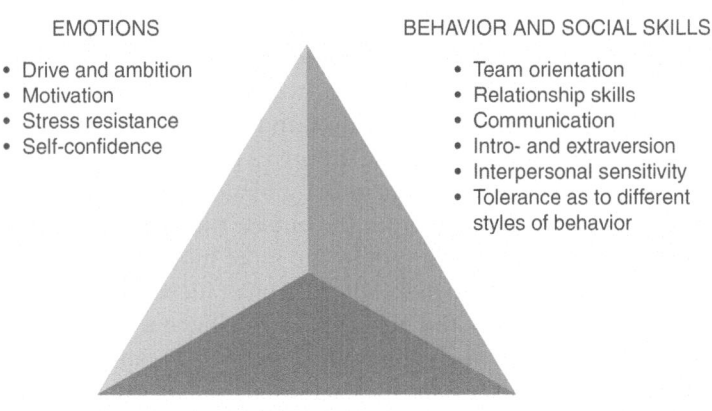

THINKING
- Strategic orientation
- Cross-cultural understanding
- Ability to deal with ambiguity and complexity
- Traditional versus innovation
- Entrepreneurial versus building systems
- Dealing with diversity

Figure 3.1 **The psychological dimensions of the Culture Shock Triangle**

combination of individual assessments, team development, workshops and follow-ups over a period of nine months.

International capability and team orientation of each executive and the team as a whole were assessed using the model of developing global leaders based on the Culture Shock Triangle (Marx 2004). This model of global leadership proposes that to be internationally effective, we have to deal with the culture shock in business, i.e. the confrontation with diversity, in three areas. There are a number of psychological dimensions related to these three areas.

The Culture Shock Triangle (Figure 3.1) provides a psychological and pragmatic framework for global leadership development. Failures in international business are often due to organizations, teams and individuals not being able to cope with culture shock in international business.

Top teams often show high levels of emotion, including anger and aggression. The present team showed scapegoating, blaming and negative personal comments. Becoming aware of these emotions in oneself and in others and the ability to manage negative emotions are key steps in achieving effectiveness in international work. Instead of responding angrily with "why don't they work like us", we should fully expect these differences, approach them openly and with curiosity and, ideally, make it an interesting challenge to deal with them. This obviously does not always work in high-pressure situations but there is a necessity to manage these emotions better. Stress and negative emotions affect our thinking in a negative way; they restrict our view, result in tunnel vision and often in non-adaptive thinking. In international teams, this leads to the situation where stereotypical behavior becomes even more pronounced, the Germans become more German, the Americans more American and French more French.

Negative mood has a strong effect on problem-solving and results in less effective solutions, both with interpersonal situations and analytical problems. As increasing market complexity demands greater creativity, every business leader should be highly alert to their own emotions, how they manage them and the impact they can create. They also need to manage the emotions and mood of the team. For example, a team of Type A executives (i.e. fast, impatient, with high drive and competitive) is less likely to find creative solutions if it is not managing the tensions it automatically produces due to its high competitiveness. This may have been what happened in the present case study.

Assessment and development

Individual development sessions with a combination of structured interviews, personality questionnaires and feedback were arranged with each executive; each session took one day. Further feedback included a confidential report and recommendations of what the individual team member needed to do to improve their own international effectiveness and their behavior in the team. Beyond the individual results, the group aggregate of all profiles showed the team's global capability, its strengths and weaknesses (in relation to the elements of the Culture Shock Triangle) and the differences in business cultures or nationalities that may occur. This greatly facilitates the understanding of cultural differences in the team. Therefore, a psychological assessment allows us to establish the following:

▷ The individual profile of international executives – how international are they and where do they need to improve?
▷ The cross-cultural differences in the team – do the different nationalities show different profiles?
▷ The cross-cultural business differences – do we find marked differences in business approaches between London and New York?

Table 3.2 Key steps to successful global team development

Step 1:	Pre-workshop questionnaire
Step 2:	One-day individual development sessions with each executive regarding their international capability and team behavior
Step 3:	• team observation • team profile • strengths and weaknesses in the team • profile of sub-teams
Step 4:	Team workshops and follow-up • presentation of team results • interactive workshops over six months • increased focus on communication and cultural differences in the team • follow-up internally to make sure that action steps are all implemented

Table 3.3 Checklist: What is your own potential as a global leader?

Questions to ask yourself

Sensitivity to different cultures
- Would others describe you as open to different ways of thinking and acting?
- Do you have a natural curiosity about foreign places?
- How culturally aware and knowledgeable are you?
- How much do you read about global business, politics and other sectors?
- How wide is your interest range?

Adaptability to new situations
- Do you quite like the challenge of ambiguous and unstructured business situations?
- Do you prefer clear-cut systems or do you like to keep things fluid and a bit vague?
- Are you proactive or even adventurous about new situations or do you like to think things through for a long time?
- How good are your communication skills?
- How are your language skills and your aptitude for learning new languages?

People orientation
- Would you describe yourself as more introvert or extravert?
- Are you a natural networker, enjoying meeting many new people?
- How empathetic are you as a leader or team member?
- What would others say about your listening skills and interpersonal sensitivity?
- Where would you place yourself on an assertiveness scale from 1 (not at all) to 7 (highly assertive)?
- How team-oriented are you really?
- What is your preferred leadership style and what have the 360° feedback reports shown about you?
- How effective are you as a negotiator and what is your style of influencing?

Resilience and ability to deal with stress
- Are you extremely self-confident, averagely so or are you a worrier and perfectionist?
- Do you get easily affected by stressful situations?
- How balanced is your life?
- Have you learnt effective ways to cope with pressure and stress?

Self-reliance
- How good is your ability to make decisions and operate independently?
- How do you manage to pull the team together whilst being self-reliant at the same time?

This global team approach ensures that the development is embedded in the strategic framework. In other words, do we have a team with a clear enough strategy, sufficient commitment and the skills and mindset to achieve the strategy? This means that all results are interpreted in relation to the strategy, i.e. objectives of the business: increasing international deal flow, group intelligence and becoming market leader.

Individual profiles

As one would expect, we found a wide spectrum of leadership characteristics, team competence and international literacy. Many executives showed Type A behavioral patterns. The profiles indicated a number of individuals lacking interpersonal sensitivity at times and lacking flexibility to deal with ambiguity. Some executives were extremely assertive and so task oriented that they never networked inside or outside the organization and did not care too much about understanding organizational dynamics and politics. Several executives used the individual development session as a springboard for further development, either through individual coaches or business school courses. The individual sessions obviously "sensitized" and prepared all executives for the subsequent team workshops.

The Psychological Component

The aggregated team profile showed many strengths, explaining why this team was successful so far; the team was highly driven, had an entrepreneurial and innovative attitude, a high focus on goals plus a high pace – all excellent characteristics to deliver results. Moreover, they were good decision-makers and showed strong leadership drives. However, the flip side was that task-oriented and self-sufficient executives with high-leadership drives tend to be poor team players. Ambition and competitiveness can make a culture where individuals try to improve their own position at the expense of their peers and the team. Traits that make individuals high achievers are not necessarily those that make them work together.

Today's business demands the brilliance associated with individualistic achievers, the "star performers", and the collective greatness associated with genuine team players. This is a particular conundrum for financial services firms, which over decades have promoted and rewarded star performers and individualists. "Individual players" reach the top, only to find that globalization requires a more team-oriented and networked approach to succeed. But similar trends are also apparent in other sectors: many teams I have worked with fall short of the task for which they were employed, i.e. finding solutions to challenges that needed collective problem-solving. Members of executive teams are often reluctant to step out of their functional or divisional role and expertise and engage in larger strategic topics. It often seems as if they do not want to take a leap into the unknown and comment on areas they are not technically "expert in". Yet it is only this type of leap that can achieve collective problem-solving.

Dysfunctional communication pattern

Initial and subsequent observations of the team in its normal working mode further proved the point. The team did not seem very functional: there was little two-way communication, with executives voicing their opinions but not engaging in dialogue. Some were short with their colleagues, blamed each other for specific problems with clients and became quite aggressive when challenged – there was certainly not much focus on collectively addressing client issues and finding a solution. The business leader also oscillated between asserting authority and direction and letting the team drift into rudderless discussions.

Ineffective thinking

The psychological assessment showed that the team needed a great deal of structure and certainty, which did not sit well with international deal-making where flexibility and an ability to cope with ambiguous scenarios is called for. Most importantly, the team had taken its eyes off its clients and off the competition – it did not have sufficient external focus. The internal tensions distracted the team from developing new clients and from focusing on the external market. To put it another way, when you are worried about the person next door scheming against you, you probably take your eye off the competition. The dysfunction in the team did not make any innovation possible. Overall, the behavior of the team was clearly not in line with the strategy of becoming market leader.

The Cultural Component

*The effect of business cultures:
The New York–London Divide*

Whilst the psychological findings were what one might expect, the cultural findings were rather surprising. One might reasonably expect the cultural differences to have arisen from the national differences between Americans and the British. Instead, the differences we found were bound to business cultures. Executives of different nationalities in London and New York had adapted to the respective local business culture. By and large, the London team were more group oriented; they debated more, collaborated more and took a more collective approach but they were also more process oriented. Communication was often a little indirect and sometimes with humor. To their New York-based counterparts, this approach seemed unnecessarily slow; they thought that London "tiptoed around issues" rather than addressing them by speaking plainly. In contrast, the New York part of the team was "highly individualistic", the members looked for quick fixes and solutions and needed to dominate proceedings; they were more self-sufficient and independent but also transaction oriented and more risk taking. To the London team, they seemed "too gung-ho" and reckless – inclined to jump to conclusions without proper reflection and process.

Beyond the differences between London and New York, there was also the functional divide between the transactors versus the business developers. Contrasting the personality types of the two groups explained some of these tensions: the transactors were more dominant and "bold" than the developers – the opposite to what one might expect for the roles. To provide effective client solutions, the sub-teams needed to work seamlessly together.

The Strategic Focus

Relating the team findings to the strategic objectives immediately clarified a list of tactics; these were specified in a series of workshops. The key actions included:

▷ Improving coordination between business development and transactors

▷ Increasing external focus with stronger marketing and positioning and continuous competitor analysis
▷ Better product development and stronger research & development and international client analysis and development
▷ Improving group intelligence with better information gathering, synthesis and analysis.

The workshops and follow-up

The first workshop introduced the framework for global team development and explained in detail the way it is linked to strategic aims and business results. It also shared the rationale for this more in-depth approach to global team building and the difference to other approaches the team may know and have experienced in the past. But let's be realistic: the psychological approach is not immediately acceptable to hard-nosed bankers – in fact one might argue it can be counter-intuitive. As in most development interventions with teams, there are some team members who do not buy-in and may even be resistant. What makes this approach possible and effective is the link up with their ambition and objectives: to make more money through better client coverage and be Number One. Having numbers and scores of the team profiles and showing the team where it is placed on different personality, cultural and functional dimensions works with rationally driven executives.

In many ways, offering a quantitative explanation for the tensions and slight dysfunctions in the team defused the emotional scenario in the team. To change a team from a disconnected, silo-ed group to a high-performing team takes a bit of time and a planned sequence of sessions to make sure the development follows the right lines.

In the current case, we had a mix of external and internal follow-ups to ensure the action steps were implemented. The first long workshop outlined the strengths and weaknesses of the team in relation to its strategy and juxtaposed the cultural and functional differences that created the tensions. These quantitative patterns worked extremely well with these financially driven executives, as they make psychological ideas or observations tangible and pragmatic and explain their impact on the team and its performance. They quantify the diversity of the team in its thinking, behavior and emotions. This is the start to being more empathetic to different ways of doing things.

The first workshop moved quickly into an interactive mode, getting the team to plan some fundamental actions: to address the identified gaps, agree on accountabilities of planned actions, time schedules and follow-ups. Motivationally, the aim is to develop a strong commitment to the agreed actions, and for the business head to reinforce the confidence that the planned actions will get results. The agreed roadmap was then followed up over the next six to eight months with a series of shorter follow-up workshops to make sure the cultural shift in the team was taking place. Commitments are not only important at team level but also at individual level. Each team member agreed to:

▷ Identify and change two types of behavior that would contribute to better teamwork
▷ Three months after the first workshop, team members rated each other on their progress in implementing the promised behavioral changes
▷ The behavioral changes also provided the basis for a values statement for the team, which each member then cascaded down to their part of the business.

The results

The business result and financial performance of the team were phenomenal as, over the following year, the team produced a revenue increase of 60 percent measured in total dollar volume of deals mandated. In terms of world ranking, it also moved up one notch in the global league table. This was a significant outcome for the business, demonstrating the impact team interventions can have both financially and on international ranking. There was also an effect, as one may expect, on the "softer" data of team dynamics; when the team results were compared with the baseline at the start, team members described how their working environment and collaboration had improved after the intervention. They expressed fewer complaints about tensions within the team and with specific individuals, there was more joint problem-solving, and, ultimately, there was significantly less tension between London and New York.

How does the approach work?

What this team approach addresses is the fundamental disconnect in many top management teams between how the team functions and the business strategy. Giving executives an understanding of their psychological make-up, the context in which they are working and their impact on others are key to bridging this divide. The psychological assessment makes the psychological diversity of the team transparent in its positive and negative ways. It also pinpoints the problem areas so that highly targeted solutions can then be developed to solve these problems. The approach works well with curious and challenging executives who are prepared to look at themselves and others in more depth.

Table 3.4 outlines a Top Team Health Check, which allows teams to take a quick check of their status and health.

Top Team Health Check

Table 3.4 Top Team Health Check

Business imperatives
- Is the team newly formed and does it need to speed up performance?
- Is the team threatened by external competition?
- Is there a change of strategy or business goals?
- Is there a need for turnaround?
- Have business targets increased significantly?
- Is the business engaging in much greater internationalization?

Alignment with culture and strategy
- Does the team have the right skills to implement the strategy?
- Is the organizational culture conducive to team performance including rewards?
- Does the team have sufficient understanding of global business issues and global clients?
- Is there agreement on strategy?
- Is the strategy specific enough?
- Is there a shared understanding on how to do business and implement the strategy?

Team effectiveness and dynamics

Emotional
- How driven, motivated and energetic is the team?
- What is the predominant mood in the team?
- What is the level of anxiety, hostility and tension?

(continued)

Table 3.4 Continued

Thinking
- International literacy: is the team able to outline different cultural perspectives?
- Is it open to different ways of thinking?
- Does it have strong knowledge of the business cultures it is operating in?
- Does it have the ability to move away from an ethnocentric stance?
- Is the team able to think on its feet and adapt to new situations?
- Does it show flexibility and the ability to deal with ambiguity?

Social behavior
- How good is the team at sharing information and knowledge?
- Is there sufficient joint problem-solving and development of group intelligence?
- What is the extent of internal and external networking?
- Is there sufficient trust and respect?
- Is there a scapegoating or blame culture?
- How much empathy do the leader and the team show?
- How many team members try to push their own agenda rather than working towards a common goal?
- Are there any domineering team members?
- How does the leader balance the need to show authority whilst instilling a consultative style and team spirit?

When to use this approach

Case 3.1 showed a way to shift a group of executives from an individualistic approach to a "networked" and globally oriented one. The Top Team Health Check already gives some indication as to when such an approach is productive:

▷ In newly formed teams to speed up performance
▷ In teams of high diversity
▷ When the team is threatened by massive external competition
▷ When there is a change of ownership, such as private equity, and a cultural shift is required
▷ Any substantial change in strategy or business goals
▷ Significant problems in the team, including tensions, competition and territorial behavior
▷ When diversity is a major obstacle rather than a source of innovation.

As was touched upon before, one of the challenges in financial services is the cult of the Star Performer. In the past, star performers could often operate in their geographic or product silos – this is no longer the case. How can we create global teams that may comprise a number of star performers?

Star Performers and How to Manage Them: Francois Curiel and Rory Sutherland

Every industry sector has star performers, whether it is financial services and its top dealmakers, the creative industry and its copywriters, or top engineers in Formula One. But how do organizations and leaders manage their star performers effectively? How do they successfully integrate them in the team so that they do not follow their own track as corporate prima donnas? How do they retain star performers whom everyone in their sector wants and probably approaches with attractive offers many times? The following interviews with business leaders in international auction and advertising companies show some of these challenges and how to manage them.

The Auction Business

Interview with Hong Kong-based François Curiel, Chairman of Christie's Asia, the international auction house:

François Curiel has had a long-standing career with Christie's, which he joined in 1969 in London as an assistant jewelry specialist, progressing quickly to senior management positions with major international roles in London, Madrid, New York, Geneva, Paris and Hong Kong. Today, as President of Christie's Asia and global chief jewelry expert, he is a star performer himself and his views are reflected in newspapers around the world. He is recognized as a top international jewelry expert and business developer, while at the same time leading a major geographical segment of Christie's business in the Asia Pacific region. Given his background, he has a unique insight into the challenges of managing star performers.

How did your own international career develop from being an expert to being a leader?
In 1976, I was asked to move to New York from Paris, where I was working as Christie's jewelry specialist, in order to open a jewelry

department there and set up a saleroom for Christie's. At the time, a head of department was essentially responsible for cataloguing the jewels, putting together the auction brochure and spending most of the time closeted in the office conducting valuations, gemmological tests and research. But I quickly realized that I was more interested in going out to get business, dealing with buyers and sellers and improving our overall presentation to make the auction process more "user and retail friendly". I hired a gemmologist with strong technical skills, who was able to handle the daily valuations and focus on writing the catalogue descriptions. Meanwhile, I worked on building a network of contacts amongst private collectors and professionals throughout the US, while introducing new ideas to present the jewelry in our catalogues; I also "invented" travelling exhibitions where we would show the jewelry in a city other than that where the auction took place. In many ways, this shift in responsibilities helped redefine the position of the Head of Department more broadly, as a business person with an active role in marketing and client development.

How do you manage star performers in a global team?
Twenty star performers, 21 ways in which to manage them. I believe the essential step is to identify what makes each executive "tick" and what is most important to them in their work. This requires a certain amount of psychology and is quite fascinating on a human level. Some colleagues need a lot of attention, others prefer to be left alone and made to feel independent. Some enjoy personal conversations, others are extremely discreet. So what I do is to remain close to all star performers and take a personal interest in them individually. I also never take them for granted, as I know that our competitors have their eyes on our best people. I also try to always remain ahead of the game, in terms of salary and career aspirations, as well as any support they may need. This is what will help build over time a relationship of loyalty and trust. Finally, if there is at any point a problem, I react quickly, not to let unanswered questions or negative feelings settle. In the auction industry, there are no schools or university which grant degrees to our future managers, so the biggest challenge is not only finding the stars and training them but also keeping them. Contrary to many other industries, we were for a long time in a duopoly in a highly competitive environment. With the arrival of our Chinese competitors, the environment is becoming even more competitive and I believe personal care and attention are key. In the end, if you ask me to sum it up in one, or rather three words, I will tell you "TLC" [Tender Loving Care].

How do you ensure that the stars are team oriented?
Having the best team means putting together a group of "real pros", who are the top experts in their area and field. These executives, who

are sometimes prima donnas, often have strong personalities and can be a little individualistic. I work with them to develop a close team spirit and introduce a global perspective. This is done through regular internal meetings and seminars, which must be productive and results driven. It is also nurtured through one-on-one conversations, simply by staying closely in touch. This was much easier 20 years ago when Christie's was smaller and more concentrated in geographic terms. In the global world, it means remaining available early in the morning till late at night, in order to speak as regularly as possible in their (not my) time zone.

If a particular colleague cannot function well as an international team member, we will identify another senior member in the department who will act as a "go-between", representing the star performer in group meetings and relaying to him or her discussions and decisions. The idea being to respect the qualities and shortcomings of our best colleagues.

From my experience, executives who perform particularly well in international teams are those with a great ability to listen and who are sensitive to a multicultural environment. It is all too easy to get stuck in an ivory tower, lost in strategies and theories, which do not correspond to the reality in the field. A good team spirit can be established if colleagues feel one understands their specific situation and can therefore offer the appropriate support and advice.

What are the key challenges in managing international teams in your sector and in the different regions your company is operating in?

▷ To be available for colleagues all over the world nearly 24 hours a day, even on holidays. I definitely do not believe in "out-of-office messages" if one wants to run a successful international team! Easy to talk about it with you, a bit more difficult in practice if you want to keep a certain balance with your private life
▷ To put myself in the shoes of the colleague asking for help or advice, regardless of my background and the cultural environment in which I work. To understand the peculiarities of his or her situation and respond accordingly
▷ To always provide a precise answer to any question, rather than being vague or, worse, not answer at all. To be able to take a decision, even if it is not always perfect and may not suit everyone. In large companies, there are often too many colleagues who are scared of making a wrong move. A good leader should be ready to take a stand.

What are the major lessons managing international teams for 20 years?
First of all, 20 years ago, managing an international team at Christie's meant mostly dealing with 1000 colleagues between London and New York. Today, we are 2500 based in 56 cities on four continents. So the

recipe is different. Twenty years ago, I would always react immediately to a problem; now, I will typically acknowledge there is an issue and wait before I react. I will prefer to sleep on it first and then make a decision. Secondly, I now realize the fundamental importance of succession planning. Whether in Paris, in Asia or in the jewelry department, I have coached potential successors and gradually shifted responsibilities into their hands. Just to take one example, in the world of jewelry, I asked the person who I believe will take over from me the reins of this department (in 200 years of course) to be the auctioneer for part of the very famous Elizabeth Taylor auction in New York in December 2011. To be seen holding the gavel during this major event (the largest jewelry auction ever organized in the world) sends a great message to the incumbent that he is highly considered by his peers and the public. So, in this case, the message is clear who the obvious leader of this section shall be. Thus, if tomorrow I fall under the proverbial No. 3 bus, the continued success of Christie's jewelry team will be guaranteed. I am in the process of doing the same thing in Asia. Lastly, I probably think more globally nowadays than 20 years ago, when I was based in the US. Most of the decisions I make today are made bearing in mind that we operate globally.

Rory Sutherland

Similar themes emerge in the advertising sector, as the following interview with Rory Sutherland, the Vice-Chairman of Ogilvy & Mather in the UK, shows.

Rory Sutherland read Classics at Cambridge, before joining Ogilvy as a Graduate Trainee in 1988. However, as the world's least organized Account Handler, after 18 months, in June 1990, he changed direction and became a copywriter.

He has worked on Amex, BT, Compaq, Microsoft, IBM, BUPA, easyJet and Unilever, winning a few awards along the way. He was appointed Creative Director of OgilvyOne in 1997 and ECD in 1998. In 2005 he was appointed Vice-Chairman of the Ogilvy Group in the UK. Rory was also elected President of the Institute of Practitioners in Advertising in 2009 for two years.

By a stroke of luck, Rory used the Internet as early as 1987. Instead of using his combined knowledge of marketing and technology to make a fortune, Rory became the first Briton to have his credit card details stolen online, thereby losing £22.45.

He is a keen proponent of behavioral economics, a subject on which he writes, speaks and tweets. In 2012 he was awarded an Honorary Doctorate of Letters by Brunel University. He is the Technology

Correspondent of the *Spectator* and a collection of his writings, *The WikiMan*, was published in 2011.

What are the key challenges in global teams?
It is absolutely vital to have a company culture that transcends the national culture. If you pick up the phone to Lisbon, Paris or London, you get a consistent approach, vocabulary and attitude. It means you identify colleagues as "Ogilvy people" first rather than as nationalities; this does not mean that there are not certain cultural variations, but consistent values and behaviors must transcend them.

The culture also requires a high element of reciprocity – there is very collegial behavior when you get requests from other offices. This is similar to the culture at firms like Goldman Sachs which, I have heard, distinguishes the firm from many other banks. It is a kind of "social capital"; an intangible asset which describes the intangible aspects of culture.

How do you create a culture where global teams work effectively together and you have this code of reciprocity?
Ogilvy is quite unique in that it had a characterful founder who created an extraordinary legacy. Essentially, David Ogilvy was instrumental in creating a classier and more intelligent approach to advertising and this is reflected in the cultural template of the company. In many important everyday questions, we do implicitly wonder what David Ogilvy would do – behavior that does not fit in to this cultural template does not work. In some sense, it is tribal, meaning if people are dissonant, they often feel the need to leave.

What will create the right behavior?
One of the big mistakes is to rely on organizational incentivizing to create the right behavior. I think much of what goes on between people is implicit and cannot be regulated by compensation only. If you have a culture of trust and reciprocity, it works much better. To give you an example of this cultural dimension: a survey from the Lisbon office just landed on my desk, informing me that they are pitching for a particular piece of work and asking me to fill in a questionnaire ascertaining what all the different Ogilvy offices have done in this area, with the intention that a strong international team approach will win the business. Knowing they will do the same for me, I have many of these requests landing on my desk and could get to the point of throwing them into the waste paper basket, but in the spirit of reciprocity, I will respond to the request as it will help the overall business.

What do you consider as key success criteria for international client work?
What you clearly notice is that some of our employees love international client work, others get frustrated by it. I ask myself sometimes whether

the British do it better than the Americans, for example, or vice-versa. My view is that the US has more of a culture of standardization whereas the British are probably more variegated.

Are there national differences regarding international client work?
Although there is a risk of stereotyping, what I have observed at Ogilvy & Mather is that some cultures are much keener on a global role or global assignments than others. The Dutch, Scandinavians and Brits have a larger appetite for international assignments than most.

What helps to pull global teams together?
In our sector, apart from the unavoidable occasional rivalry, people work very well together; everyone has high intrinsic interests, which is helpful. Most talented people are not motivated by self-enrichment alone. And this is different from some of the financial services cultures where someone's gain is seen to come at someone else's expense.

What is your advice for team leaders?
Creative people are difficult to manage – it is not a job where there are right answers in any case. The ability to manage depends on your professional reputation in large part. This is quite similar to software development; you need to be to the best coder in the building first.

How do you manage the stress in international work?
Working with people in different time zones has its challenges. Sometimes it is frustrating to have to go for a three-day trip to Chicago just because your presence could be useful for 20 minutes. But there is also a clear danger of travel addiction. Travel addiction sets in because you badly need those six hours in the air to catch up on your e-mails. I think it was Emile Durkheim who created the term "anomie risk". This job is not like building a wall – in our work, we may have no feedback for months. Sometimes at the end of the day with all the e-mails and phone calls, I do not really know what I have done or what I have achieved. I feel as if I have moved a pebble but I am not sure towards what final end I have moved it. What board leadership needs to do is to provide people with a clear sense of meaning. Leaders need to create a narrative around the various actions, and a lot of today's organizational practices, particularly the overly metrics-obsessed approaches, actually destroy this wider sense of purpose. It can make people resentful towards their employer.

This last point is a well-known finding of how an overreliance on metrics can actually erode intrinsic motivation and undermine the performance of individuals and teams.

3 ▶ GLOBAL TEAMS

Chapter 3 showed how international teams can work together more successfully by taking the key components of the Culture Shock Triangle into consideration, focusing on emotions, thinking and behavior. Often top teams respond faster to the thinking component of this model. They can apply the experience with their day-to-day work and understand the basics of different business cultures.

Chapter 4 will look more closely at the challenge of change: whether it is the change to a more performance-oriented culture or the challenge of international mergers. It also looks more closely at the process of team development and what one ideally needs to do to build resilience for change, and manage resistance and conflict situations that may occur. The case study is based on a European consumer company and illustrates the necessity of getting the basics right in terms of team and behavioral governance.

4 Driving Change, Growth and Innovation

A couple of years ago, I was asked by a European company to coach one of its top executives who was in the process of integrating a merger of two European businesses. The company had a strong reputation for its professionalism and consequently the merger was assiduously planned; human resource preparation was diligent in order to ensure a smooth integration and use the synergies between the businesses effectively. Yet, six months after the merger was announced, many executives of the acquired organization had left of their own volition, the business performance dropped and the Divisional CEO was asked to work with an external consultant to stabilize the international team, reduce the number of defections and focus on the development of the top team.

When I traced the merger history and the pre-merger activities, I found extremely valuable information on the cultures of the two merging organizations: they did not differ simply in terms of nationality but in organizational cultures and processes. An extensive and expensive merger assessment had been carried out, outlining clearly the many compatibilities of the two businesses, their cultural synergies, but also showing significant risk areas. The number of compatibilities clearly outweighed the number of risk areas or incompatibilities, ergo the consulting firm concluded with positive predictions as to the merger's success. Yet the reality was different six months on: the second stage of the merger did not look too successful. What had happened?

▷ Whilst the risk areas were fewer than the number of synergies, they were psychologically significant and their importance was not highlighted in the original report

▷ The consultancy was very good at diagnostics but probably not as good at offering help in the implementation stage; the client was left to work this out on their own
▷ The company had an excellent human resource due-diligence and merger preparation process, but this stopped when the deal was completed – it concentrated on the "hardware" of the deal but not on the "software" of making it work.

The process of change is often neglected in favor of the "hardware" or tangible factors. If businesses want to grow, produce a turnaround or innovate, they need to understand and manage the process of change, the "software", better, from the top level down. This chapter looks at the process of change, starting with mergers and then focusing on a specific team development that transformed a stagnating business into a profitable one.

International Mergers – The Shock of the Alien

Before the financial crisis of 2008, international mergers reached a record high. Whilst we are currently still in a rather paralytic phase as far as mergers are concerned, this is bound to change – and also bound to change with respect to "merger initiators", as more and more Asian organizations are acquiring companies in Europe, such as Tata's acquisitions of Jaguar Land Rover in 2008. As we know, many mergers never achieve the projected business success. We know that differences in leadership style between the merging companies, and particularly in areas such as attitudes towards risk, affect the company results negatively. What happens when different organizational cultures collide: what is the effect on employees, their morale and performance over time?

In many ways, the effect of culture shock or "the shock of the alien" is seen on a much larger scale as it affects the entire organization. When talking to executives who have been through company mergers, they report experiences that are totally incongruent with the positive rhetoric of the merger announcement: they find it stressful, particularly because of the high anxiety about job losses. Moreover, the underlying rationale for mergers – with the ultimate aim of creating better shareholder value is typically put into question by significant falls in shareholder value over the longer term.

The failure of international mergers may be the direct result of culture shock, which, as we have seen, is similar to the shock individuals experience when posted abroad for the first time – feelings of foreignness, "otherness" or the unfamiliar. Individuals go through a process of adaptation when working in a new culture, oscillating between positive and negative phases before adapting. In my view, merging organizations go through similar phases, ranging from a honeymoon phase to a period of culture shock to eventual adaptation.

Senior executives, especially the top team and board who are driving the merger, enjoy the privilege of a *honeymoon phase*: they are very positive about the merger and pronounce its advantages, internally and externally. But employees lower down the hierarchy typically miss out on the positive emotions of the "merger honeymoon", plunging straight in to the negative emotions of culture shock: they fear they will lose their job, particularly where concurrent redundancy programs result from the merger, are uncertain as to what role they may have, and often feel helpless. As a high-flying banker commented on her experience of a banking merger, "I envied every staff member down to the porter who had a sense of purpose and knew what his job was about."

The ongoing uncertainty has psychological and organizational consequences. The individual will spend most of their working time worrying, envying "'the porter" and anyone who has a "sense of purpose", and trying to interpret organizational politics.

Consequently, not much time is spent on the task at hand or previously agreed deliverables. There is an excessive internal focus on trying to read the politics of the new organization – mostly reflected in the key appointments of the new board and senior team – and not many executives give the external world and competitors much time and energy. As a result, there is paralysis of productive activity and the merged company can run into performance problems straight away and/or have major defections of well-regarded staff who follow more secure offers from competitors. Depending on the quality of the leadership at the top in managing the psychological effects of the merger

4 ▶ DRIVING CHANGE, GROWTH AND INNOVATION

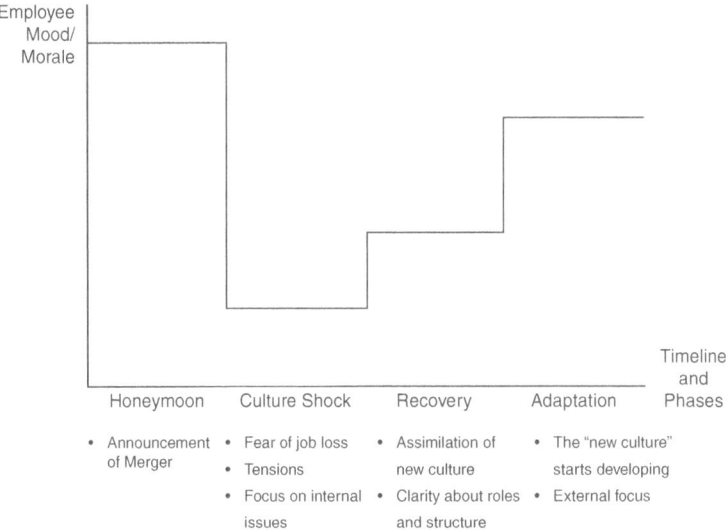

Figure 4.1 **The culture shock in mergers (after Oberg, 1960)**

on staff, employees eventually start to develop a more realistic and productive view of the merger. For example, they might see the scope for more interesting roles, international assignments, and ways to improve their skill base and career potential. Over time, and depending on the capability of the leaders to manage the new teams, a "recovery phase" occurs, when teams start to integrate and assimilate new values, attitudes and working styles.

In an ideal world, this is the time when a compromise and the development of new values, attitudes and behaviors starts, and when the "new culture" starts to emerge. If leaders spent as much time on the human "due diligence" as they typically spend on the financial one, we may see much better business performance in mergers. Accountants should pay attention to the following: business performance, as reflected in shareholder value, seems to follow exactly the same pattern as the cultural adaptation curve in Figure 4.1. The typically high shareholder value after a merger announcement is often replaced by a drastic drop when the lack of synergies, cultural clashes and internal problems arise, before moving to an improved shareholder value later on.

Creating a New Culture

"The state of the company was much worse than I anticipated and I knew I had to make some fast changes to achieve a turnaround."

"The organization had not produced any profits for six years and I found a huge team of 20 executives at the top – it was obvious that the company needed to change its culture."

"We know Asia and South America are the key growth markets for our future – however, we are still a very Eurocentric organization and need to become a real global one fast."

These are the comments of chief executives I have spoken to in the course of my consulting activities.

"Change" and "change management" are overused words and seem to apply to most organizational activities nowadays. We find a large number of work streams, projects and elaborate coordinations, often supported by strategy and change management consultants. Many of these projects are implemented at the mid-level of organizations, with the top of the organization only touched by strategic updates. But change starts at the top, with the understanding, attitudes and behavior of the CEO/business leader and the top team. A merger is an extreme example of cultural change, driven by overt, external events and structural change necessities. Many cultural changes are not as "high octane" or under the same public limelight. They are often less overt, more subtle and under less external scrutiny. The premise here is that if you want to change the culture of an organization, you need to start with the culture at the top, or the psychology of the top team. If the culture is the "software of the mind", we need to understand more about the psychology or "software" at the top of organizations.

What happens at group level? Key elements to focus on are:

▷ Providing a good emotional baseline and improving resilience
▷ Enhancing interpersonal relations and communication, as well as cultural understanding.

Berry et al. (2002), in their seminal book on cross-cultural psychology, differentiate between *psychological adaptation* and *socio-cultural adaptation* in international groups and teams. The different timelines of these adaptation processes have direct practical implications for improving international team effectiveness, suggesting business leaders should focus on the emotional stability of the team and develop a good "emotional baseline" before doing anything else!

According to Berry et al., psychological issues often increase soon after contact with people who are very different, followed by a general decrease over time. This is consistent with the emotional aspects of the Culture Shock Triangle, where emotional problems and stress can flare up in international teams. The level and extent of the problems depend on personality variables, such as emotional stability and resilience, external stress, such as increased competition or economic crisis, the style of the leader, as well as the social support available in its widest sense. The CEO or business leader needs to be highly alert to psychological issues occurring and, ideally, try to pre-empt them by focusing on the resilience aspect of individuals and the team.

The socio-cultural adaptation typically has a linear improvement over time. Essentially, the more contact, the better the socio-cultural adaptation, which also applies to any form of team development and time spent together, whether inside or outside the office. Berry et al found that good socio-cultural adaptation is predicted by cultural knowledge, the degree of contact and positive inter-group attitudes. This supports the organization's attempt to ensure sufficient cultural preparation for their teams.

Nevertheless, whilst we see some good practices to facilitate the socio-cultural adaptation of teams, there is insufficient focus on the management of emotions in teams – even though this is essential for progress and delivery.

Case 4.1: Accelerating a Turnaround

Transforming a stagnating business into a profitable one

Case 4.1

A European consumer company that was slow and bureaucratic and had too many layers of management needed a drastic cultural

> change. Essentially, it had become an outmoded organization – it was not sufficiently customer oriented and had to become more performance oriented.
>
> The business was under pressure as it had not produced any significant profits for several years and was seen as colossal, with too many management levels and an oversized board that was not reaching any decisions. A new CEO was appointed, who started to make immediate changes to his executive team. He threw a bombshell by immediately reducing the team size and replacing many of its members. These were strong signs, internally and externally, of significant changes; however, these changes also resulted in uncertainty and stress throughout the organization. The new CEO was intuitive and aware of this but, equally, he was extremely driven and felt an urgency to introduce a more positive, innovative and customer-oriented culture that was performance oriented and not weighed down by bureaucratic hierarchies. This had to start at the top, with himself and the senior team, and he knew that he could accelerate the cultural change working with an external consultant.
>
> The CEO immediately engaged a consultant to start some top team development. The consultant ran a team workshop but for some reason their approach did not work in bringing the team together. By the time I met the CEO, I was not sure whether the timing for an effective team intervention had already passed and whether another attempt could have real credibility and impact. The first attempt seemed to have consisted of a well-planned workshop but without planning the longer term process of change.

The approach

It was decided that a different, more in-depth psychological and longitudinal approach was needed; one that would also help the individual executive to understand his/her role better in driving the change agenda, before extending the approach to the entire team and then throughout the organization.

As the changes ultimately needed to affect the entire organization, a systemic, governance-oriented approach was required, complementing the psychological one.

A psychological approach on its own would not have been effective to switch a bureaucratic team culture to a more dynamic

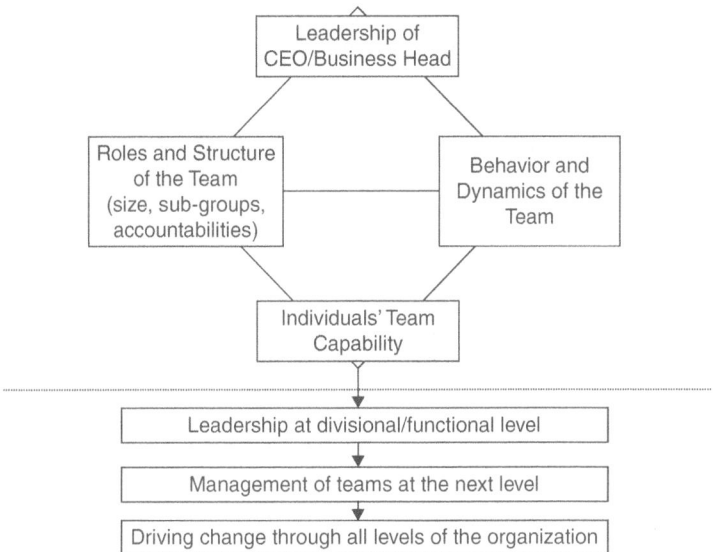

Figure 4.2 **Team development and systemic change**

and customer-oriented one. Different team governance was also needed. As outlined in Chapter 2, we can differentiate between three levels of team development. The initial assessment of the team status (as shown in the Top Team Health Check), the objectives, and the culture of the organization will determine the priorities of or balance between the different levels of team development. All three levels should ideally be considered, and in this company it was decided a combination of governance (Level I) and psychological development (Level III) would be effective.

The upper half of Figure 4.2 shows that it is often not sufficient to focus on the psychological dynamics of the team – the structure and roles of the team and the CEO's style have fundamental influences on the effectiveness and performance of the team. The impact of leadership styles on team effectiveness is explored in more detail in Chapter 6. The lower half of Figure 4.2 suggests looking at individual executives in two ways: their behavior within teams and as leaders of their own teams.

The second aspect is paramount in aligning the top team's strategy with the teams at the next level and in driving the change agenda throughout the organization. A combination of individual and team development has impact because it helps every executive to improve both their functional role and their own capability to be a team player.

Team Governance

Team governance or "team basics", such as structure, accountabilities and roles in the team, need to be clear for it to function well. Team governance is well addressed in Katzenbach and Smith's practical model of team performance. As a reminder, they define a team as "a small number of people with complementary skills who are committed to a common purpose, performance goals and approach for which they hold themselves mutually accountable" (1993, p.45).

If all the elements in the above definition are met, we should have a good level of team effectiveness and a real team. Beyond these conditions, high-performance teams have one more ingredient that is hard to engineer: they are interested in each other's growth and wellbeing (beyond their professional roles) and they have high personal chemistry – often seen in special project teams.

More realistically, most team interventions aim to develop real, i.e. effective, teams. In order to achieve this, Katzenbach and Smith suggest a number of steps that would help any leader to improve team performance:

▷ Select members based on technical and interpersonal skills – team assessment
▷ Establish urgency, challenge and direction
▷ Pay attention to first meetings and actions
▷ Set clear rules of behavior
▷ Set performance-oriented tasks and goals
▷ Challenge the group regularly
▷ Spend a lot of time together
▷ Reward properly.

What Happens in Practice?

The state of governance in executive teams

Considering Katzenbach and Smith's recommendations, my experience working with senior teams in different countries attests to the following realities:

▷ Many top teams are built in an ad-hoc way. Business leaders get a sense of everyone's capability within a few months of working together, but this rarely amounts to a more objective review of skills.
▷ Urgency and challenges are evident in most businesses, but these are often exerted by external forces; in other words, what is the balance between reactivity and proactivity in a team?
▷ The first meetings are normally extremely well planned and executed, as most leaders use this as the ideal platform to energize and motivate the new team and to establish themselves. Follow-ups in terms of longitudinal discipline are often less well established.
▷ Understandably, no one wants to talk about "rules" at the top level or about "behavioral expectations"; it smells of entry-level inductions. Nevertheless, discussing productive and results-oriented team behavior is helpful, particularly in international teams where expectations and attitudes about effective behavior can be wildly different. As we will see later, the cultural ideals of interpersonal skills vary enormously and can be a stumbling block if team members are not aware of this.
▷ Goal setting is usually a forte in executive teams – but psychological assessments show that many executives are inclined to set objectives in an over-specific way, leaving little room to maneuver and adapt to changing circumstances.

It is a good mini-exercise to check whether there is a common understanding of the strategy and its primary goals. Ask eight executives in a team to write down the strategic objectives and you will get eight different answers. With this type of result, the CEO often shows his/her frustration, restating that he/she has given three strategy presentations and that they have had extensive discussions – yet, there is still no common understanding because of subjective interpretations and selective listening. This hints at the challenge of "bringing strategy alive" by creating meaning and engagement. Neil Berkett, the Chief Executive of Virgin Media, has done this very successfully as part of his turnaround of the company, which will be reviewed later on in this chapter.

▷ Why is it so difficult for a Number One player to stay at the top long term? Does the team challenge itself and its business model enough? There are, of course, a variety of reasons but one is that the top team may rest on its success too long and follow the same, well-proven way to produce business results. At governance level, there will be well-organized team agendas, but these will often give over disproportionate amounts of time to operational as opposed to strategic issues. Moreover, the current economy has exacerbated the short-term orientation; short-term cash generation is at the forefront in many companies.

How does the team challenge itself?

At an interpersonal level, many business leaders find it hard to de-couple the two sides of challenge: the cognitive differences and the affective/interpersonal consequences. They fear full-blown conflicts in the team. Yet managing conflicts, at an intellectual and emotional level, should be a key competence of leaders: intellectually leaders need to be comfortable with paradoxes, as described in Chapter 1, and have the confidence and interpersonal skills to manage the potential "emotional fallout" and stabilize the team. Parking longer term strategy discussions to a twice yearly off-site is not effective. If teams and boards do not challenge themselves regularly, they will be challenged by the competition or the external market; it is the difference between proactive and reactive teams.

▷ Spending a lot of time together helps but how is time together well spent?

Most leaders are well aware of the benefits of spending a lot of time with their teams and doing this effectively right from the start of working with a new team. Social bonding in a team builds resilience. Research on stress has shown that social support is one of the best stress buffers and applies to all types of stressful events, including major life events such as divorce and redundancy. Within a team, spending time together will not just improve the team's dynamics but will increase its social support and resilience, thereby increasing its ability to deal with bigger challenges and changes. The best leaders stabilize their teams emotionally and focus on building resilience in their teams.

However, spending time together needs to be tailored to the needs of the specific team and there are two points a business leader may want to consider: introverts in the team and the "cultural distance" in social behavior in an international group.

Introverts, to put it simply, do not need a lot of social interaction to function effectively, as opposed to extraverts, who need social contacts to energize and motivate themselves. Extraverts love ad-hoc social interactions. They need the "water cooler" chats in the office. Introverts, by contrast, need time on their own to re-energize. They will still enjoy social interactions but fewer of them, and they are generally more comfortable in content-driven or structured social meetings rather than cocktail parties. Introverts will best adapt to a new team if off-sites are more structured and they have some time between meetings to spend on their own and energize that way.

What should a business leader know about cultural differences regarding the overlap or separation between work and personal life? These differences can have an impact on day-to-day team collaboration. As Evelyn Havasi, one of the most prominent women on Wall Street and a senior Managing Director at Citi, explained: "What I have observed is that the US is often not so sensitive to different working styles of other nationalities, whether European or Asian. I have worked with US teams who have no issues with midnight conference calls, for example, but Europeans have more boundaries about calls at unsocial times or on holidays."

Whether individuals want to mix work and personal time, whether they like spending social time with work colleagues and whether they like to divulge personal information is, of course, influenced by the individual's personality. However, there are also cultural differences in the definition and overlap of public and private space. The US is an excellent example of the large overlap between public and private space – in other words, there is little separation between the two spheres. Americans make friends easily, whether at work or outside work, they are adaptable about working on weekends and they often volunteer personal information. Contrast this with Northern Europe where there is less overlap and greater separation between the two spaces.

There are numerous other cultural differences in communication patterns, from the expression of emotion to eye contact, from the ideal type of presentation to generate interest with foreign clients to the use of humor in business. Richard Lewis, the inter-cultural expert, has explored these differences extensively in his book *When Cultures Collide* (1996). Whilst we need to be aware of some fundamental differences in social behavior, it is also important to point out the cross-cultural similarities and the universality of human behavior, as shown in the universality of emotions.

Universality of emotions

Paul Ekman, the psychologist, showed decades ago that all humans, whether Aborigines in Papua New Guinea or Wall Street bankers, experience the same set of basic emotions: happiness, fear, sadness, anger, disgust, surprise. But, equally, he showed the universality of facial expression of these emotions. When Aborigines in Papua New Guinea are shown photographs of Americans expressing different emotions (from happiness to disgust), they can correctly identify the emotions, and the same is true vice versa. We therefore have a perfect common baseline for reading the emotional responses of others throughout the world and in adapting our reactions accordingly. However, it is still necessary to appreciate what is an acceptable display of emotions in different cultures. As Ekman (1973) puts it, there are different "display values or different norms regarding the expected management of facial appearance." In an experiment with Japanese and US students, he showed the differences in the students' emotional display when they watched a stressful film firstly on their own and then with others. Whereas the American students showed much the same reaction in both settings, the Japanese students showed similar facial reactions to their American peers when watching the film on their own but much fewer facial expressions in a group situation. Hence, their emotions were hard to read in the presence of others.

We have an amazing ability to adapt to changing circumstances. As Case 3.1 showed, American bankers in London had adapted to the London business culture and showed similar reactions as their European colleagues. This *acculturation* effect is important to keep in mind for any changes we want to make in business cultures, whether this relates to cost-cutting, growth or innovation. This ability to acculturate is probably best shown in individuals who are truly bicultural or even tricultural; they have the ambidextrous ability to adapt to different cultural contexts. An example is given in Sussman and Rosenfeld's (1982) study on personal space: when speaking in their own language, Japanese students in the US seated themselves further apart from each other than students from Venezuela speaking in their own language. However, this cultural difference disappeared when speaking English: when speaking English, students from both countries sat at a similar distance as students from the US.

In fact, cross-cultural research has changed from simply juxtaposing cultural differences to exploring "culture in context". This is a more differentiated approach: it reinforces a more sophisticated approach to international business rather than a prescriptive, stereotypical framework of national or business cultures. It is this sharpening of our observation, inquiry and understanding that is required before we can progress to develop effective solutions in global business.

▷ Katzenbach and Smith's advice to "reward properly" requires an entire book analyzing current remuneration systems, individual and team components and cultural differences in reward expectations. Remuneration systems should be aligned with the goals of the team, and the team component reflects its contribution towards a common goal.

Within the Western business world, there is a sharp divide between the Anglo-Saxon (the US and UK) approach to pay, where the differentials between the pay of the CEO and the most junior employee's pay are less critically monitored, and in Northern Europe where these differentials are closely analyzed. The entitlement of an absolute, individualistic reward is clearly evident in the Global Elite – global talent can demand highly tailored packages. Rewards and metrics have long overtaken the attention to psychological contracts as retention strategies. But as many psychological studies have shown, the excessive focus on monetary and extrinsic rewards undermines exactly what it hopes to reinforce: the intrinsic interest in the work and the resulting intrinsic energy and motivation. Ogilvy's Vice-Chairman Rory Sutherland described this well in relation to the creative industry in Chapter 3

Katzenbach and Smith's recommendations to develop teams can be applied in different international contexts – they help to counteract one of the biggest risks: the excessive focus on operational activities and working as "executive silos". As Case 4.1 will illustrate, a governance framework is the backdrop for an international team-development model; it ensures that the "team basics" or team discipline are in place. This is often easiest checked with a brief team questionnaire.

Culture change

The challenge for the European consumer company was to produce significantly higher profits, and doing so required a culture change. If culture is "the way we are doing things", then culture change suggests a "reconditioning" to do things differently. Strategy consultants are called in and produce a clear map of strategic and tactical objectives. Yet, the shift in mindset and behaviors is usually not mentioned.

Similar to the merger curve at the beginning of this chapter, we could imagine a cultural change curve with the same emotional and performance consequences. In our case scenario, the executive team of eight was aware it needed to know its customers better, be more responsive to customer and market shifts, more innovative in product development, marketing and distribution, and more nimble and flexible. However, trying to shed the slow bureaucratic culture seemed a painful project – the team knew it needed to replace the hierarchical culture with a collaborative and flatter one. **The fastest way to change the culture of a business is to change the culture of the top team.** The CEO knew that changes needed to start at the top, as the top team is the role model for the rest of the business. He was intuitive and had a clear picture of what good team dynamics look like. He also had an effective interpersonal style and was well-versed in managing international teams. He was open to a more psychological approach that included individual and team development.

Team Diagnostics

Interviews with each executive and a team questionnaire showed the following results:

▷ The current team collaboration was described as "rudimentary": "We don't really work together yet, we meet together"
▷ It was still "in development" and remarks suggested a silo-orientation: "We do not have a common basis of interests or activities"; "We are closed and not open enough in communicating with each other"
▷ The main strengths of the team were seen in its technical skills (and the team had phenomenal functional expertise) and in its positive motivation and energy: "We respect each other, but we don't really work together"; "We lack a shared vision and progress on the culture and behaviors we want to see"
▷ The main weaknesses were its internal competitive thinking, a lack of clarity and insecurity. "One's role in the team is unclear"; "Which decisions are made in the team and which outside the team remain unclear"; "We need a clear operating model and more open communication where conflicts can be resolved and where honest feedback is encouraged and appreciated"
▷ On a five-point scale, team effectiveness was rated as 2.5.

The team development included:

▷ *Focus on governance*, starting with the definition of common goals, structures and expectations, then addressing the current silo mentality: "clarifying the operating model"
▷ *The development of key values* for the team and the business. "Define the behaviors we want to see and how we will get them – symbols and signals for the rest of the organization; clarify the way the team will work"; "The 'team value' in the company needs to be overt and be seen"
▷ *Building stronger interpersonal relations:* get to know each other better and communicate effectively. "We need to spend more time together, and develop more trust"
▷ *Focus on success*: after years of flagging business results, there was urgency to produce some success in the short-term.

Individual leadership development sessions

Effective team governance starts with individual governance – are individuals' roles clear in the change process? Does each executive have a vision and effective processes to run the functional or business unit? The individual development sessions looked at these questions and followed a similar process as described in Case 3.1. The one-day sessions provided concrete action plans on how to drive the turnaround from an individual perspective and had the following components:

▷ Structured career interview
▷ Personality assessment
▷ Analysis of interpersonal and work values
▷ Analysis of career values
▷ Feedback and development session
▷ Individual report, recommendations and key action plans.

Table 4.1 gives a snapshot of a development summary.

The development areas specify what the executive needs to do in his/her role to advance the cultural changes. Action steps can be related to the Culture Shock Triangle, such that the individual needs to:

1. Work on the *emotional stability* and understand what situations will trigger stress or sensitivities and what to do about them

2. *Stretch their way of looking at business* from operational to being more strategic
3. *Refine their good social skills* further by stronger cross-cultural understanding and developing "international" social skills, and complementing their style as "independent operator" with more team-oriented activities.

Team profile

The aggregate of all psychological information was shared with the team in the first development workshop, addressing the following questions:

▷ What are the strengths and weaknesses of the team in relation to the business strategy?
▷ How can potential gaps be overcome and what actions should be taken?
▷ What risk areas need to be monitored and at what interval?

Table 4.1 Example of a development summary

Strengths
- Excellent social skills and communication style
- Good ability to strike rapport and build relationships
- "Planful" and systematic approach with preference for structure
- Pragmatic and value oriented
- Relatively flexible as to methods
- Highly decisive

Development areas
- The direct interaction style could be undiplomatic in international situations
- The high need for independence does not make the executive a natural team player
- A "planful" and rather risk-averse approach will restrict growth and business development
- The pragmatic orientation, whilst positive in getting things done, does not allow space and time for strategic thinking
- Needs to be clearer in goal setting for his own role and for the team
- There is slight emotional sensitivity in the profile which could make it difficult to deal with a lot of pressure and the stress of change

The key trends of the team profile were as follows (Table 4.2):

Table 4.2 Key findings of team profile

Social behavior:
- Whilst the team profile showed overall a strong social orientation and team preparedness, the team scored high on assertiveness and dominance. This increased the risk of ongoing conflicts and power games

Thinking
- The team profile showed many strengths that were ideal for change management: a positive and proactive task approach, high flexibility and preference for new methods. However, the culture change was at risk because the team did not have a strong sensitivity or understanding of psychological issues; it was facts-and-figures oriented and did not consider sufficiently the effects of decisions on people

Emotional
- The team had a good ability to deal with the stress and pressures of a turnaround
- Team members varied in self-confidence to deal with difficult situations and the team showed a high level of tenseness, which probably reflected the pressure the team was under

Table 4.3 Team development agenda

Psychological Factors	Cultural Objectives	Strategic Objectives
• high assertiveness and competition • individual players with high self-sufficiency • low sensitivity to psychological issues • emotional tenseness	• openness and transparency • clarity in roles • clear decision-making rules • effective conflict resolution	• building a performance culture • higher customer orientation and faster pace • focus on innovation

Governance Workshops

A series of workshops and interactive sessions, where the team could discuss and agree on its governance framework and way of working together, was planned.

4 ▶ DRIVING CHANGE, GROWTH AND INNOVATION

The following are examples of some of these sessions.

Team governance – what are our common goals, accountabilities and expectations?

▷ Common goals – beyond operational focus
▷ Strategy development and communication:
   ○ When, how often and in what format?
▷ Leading change:
   ○ What does it require from us individually and as a team?
   ○ Who are the main change agents in the team?
   ○ What are effective ways to communicate and inspire change at next level down?
▷ Building a common culture that is performance oriented and "faster":
   ○ Key differences of "before" and "after"
   ○ What will stay and what will change?
▷ Developing a better customer orientation:
   ○ What are the benchmarks?
   ○ How do we evaluate our customer relations?
   ○ Sub-teams to drive this strategically and to plan implementation companywide
▷ Focus on external market:
   ○ How do we ensure a stronger external focus?
   ○ What are external monitors and relationships we need to build?

Team culture – how do we want to work together?

▷ Which decisions are made inside the team and which outside?
▷ How do we make sure that sensitive topics are discussed and in a constructive way?
▷ How do we want to deal with conflicts that come up?
▷ How do we deal with internal competition and make sure we focus on the external competition?
▷ What are key indicators of success for us – beyond metrics?
▷ What should the frequency and style of team meetings look like - operational and strategic topics?
▷ How can we support each other better and provide the emotional support needed for change?

▷ How do we make space to discuss psychological issues?
▷ How do we appear as a unified team and what are the boundaries to the next level?

Key findings

Over a period of nine months during which the workshops were implemented, the team became noticeably more aligned, which was also observed by the executives at the next level of management. The weaknesses were successfully addressed and the executives became more open with each other. Some shared their full psychological reports. The HR Director was instrumental in monitoring progress of the new governance processes. The CEO spent more time coaching each executive throughout this change process. The business results improved and the company generated a significant profit for the first time in several years.

Governance and Innovation: Thomas Geitner

Thomas Geitner was the CEO of New Business and Innovation and a former board director at Vodafone before he joined the board of the German Conglomerate Henkel as President of the Adhesives Division, with businesses all over the world. Since 2011, he has been building an international portfolio of board and advisor positions with companies in the UK, Switzerland and Germany.

How do you move from governance to real-team effectiveness?
It is useful to differentiate between two components that make effective governance: first, ensuring compliance and secondly, building trust. Compliance at board level can really only be effective if it is underpinned by strong processes throughout a business organization and a matching culture to live up to values and processes. One could say that the "internal" governance of a business provides the confidence and trust that the basic controls are reliable. It contributes to trust building. As a minimum, we need clear mechanisms for key business activities, such as budget setting, financial performance, how to react to deviations, on what principles to compete and how promotion decisions are being made. Essentially, you need to build an organization that makes business controls and people promotion transparent and can motivate any type of talent. I have worked in organizations that had dozens of international operations and an equal number of different local competitors. The philosophy in some companies is to bring up local talent in each

market to run the country operations whereas others "shoot in" their own nationals, i.e. expatriates from headquarters, and have less local talent at the top.

You have worked in international business for 30 years with some of the best brands. What are the key lessons you have learned in building international businesses through effective teams?
One of the key lessons is that you can only be successful if you have people whose capability reflects the complexity and the scale of the strategy. In other words, if you want to double the business in a region from one to two billion dollars and change its product to more complex ones, you need top executives and a team who are able to run a much larger and more complex business from the outset: you recruit for the future needs of the business; unfortunately this is often not done. You look both at the capabilities of the team and whether it instills trust and is culturally congruent with the values of the organization.

How do you develop trust?
In most companies I have worked in, the fundamental belief was to trust local management – the companies also developed sophisticated mechanisms to develop local talent through long-term grooming of key executives. Secondly, as mentioned above, introduce standardized business processes in the key control areas.

How does global product development work?
There are big differences as to whether the company is producing a real global product like Apple or locally adapted products, as is the case in many telecommunications companies. For example, if you have a great technology idea in Silicon Valley, you get a high-calibre tech team together and develop a great product which you can then put on to a scalable product idea and aim for global success. In telecommunication companies, for example, you need a mix of global and local product teams to adapt the products successfully to the specific country. Essentially, you have a model of distributed decision-making.

How do you create a more innovative organization and how do you ensure better innovation in an international team?
As soon as we are dealing with complex products which need to be continuously refined and further developed, we need to think about cultural changes in an organization. We need to question whether our organizational culture can generate innovation and adaptability of products. I have driven a lot of transformations in my career and found it very helpful to think about the cultural dimensions of hierarchical/non-hierarchical and relationship-orientation/merit dimensions. Many organizations still have a hierarchical structure where many decisions are driven by relationships rather than by merit. This does not work for

international talent in technology – they want to work in flatter structures where skills and innovation are core values and promotions are made on merit.

Essentially you need to build an organization that makes people promotion transparent and creates a level opportunity for communication and promotion.

What are the other leadership challenges for you in pulling an international team together?

One major challenge is clearly how to communicate effectively in an international context. When I originally arrived in the UK from Germany, my English was still very direct. I had a challenging communication style, which was not acceptable in a British business environment, so I had to focus and mirror the implicit British politeness in pursuing my targets to make sure others had the space to maneuver.

One has to develop effective bicultural communication and influencing skills – this is more than just knowing the language. In other regions, like Asia or the Middle East, you also have unique communication patterns to learn. The US and UK have a huge advantage as native English speakers, which clearly helps their influencing skills. There is an old saying that if you have to communicate in a non-native language, initially you need 30 percent of your intelligence for getting communication right. This raises the issue of recruitment of non-native speakers as well as the issue of promotion – who does the recruitment and how well are they prepared to assess global talent? We need to ensure that non-national talent is being recognized and this requires a culture that is sensitive to these communication issues. In some ways, the situation for non-nationals is easier in some Continental European companies that have made the decision that the company language is English. There is then a level playing field in language because, except for native English speakers, everyone has the same need to communicate in a non-native language. This creates more tolerance for non-native speakers and a very international cadre of senior executives at headquarters. This international mix at headquarters probably facilitates a different level of understanding of global talent.

Differences in business cultures

When we talk about cultural differences, we often mean national differences, Chinese nationals compared to Americans, or French to Scandinavians. But as the example of global teams in Case 3.1 showed, there are also significant differences in business cultures, which may override other differences: American executives working in London had similar working styles to British executives. It is part of *acculturation* or adaptation. Chapter 3 outlined a framework to understand cultural differences without being prescriptive or stereotyping. Similarly, when trying to change a business culture, it is useful to have a framework to understand the critical elements of past performance and behavior, and desired future performance and behavior. As Thomas Geitner explained in his interview, he found it helpful to look at the hierarchical/non-hierarchical and relationship/merit-based cultural dimensions when considering the transformations he implemented. In fact, one could argue that a mapping of the business culture should be regularly carried out, not only to manage change better but to increase the fit in recruitment. Increasing the cultural fit at the top of organizations is explored in detail in Chapter 5.

As the interview with Thomas Geitner also illustrated, telecommunication companies differ in their history, philosophy and organizational cultures. Organizations differ from each other in their beliefs and values, rituals and heroes (see Rory Sutherland's comment on David Ogilvy in Chapter 3).

Schein (1985) points out three levels to look at when trying to understand organizational cultures:

1. observable behaviors
2. values
3. unconscious basic assumptions.

The least tangible is the core of the culture: the unconscious basic assumptions. The unconscious basic assumptions of what is right and wrong in business, what constitutes talent and what behavior is desirable will determine the culture of the company and the way things are done. This also explains the inconsistencies we find in the business world, the inconsistency between the values as outlined in company reports and employee manuals and what we overtly see, as in executives' behavior day to day.

Whilst I am not proposing an "organizational psychoanalysis" to assess the unconscious assumptions, a reflection on the above issues and the inconsistency we find in organizations is useful – none more so than in the area of diversity. As experts on diversity may argue, with so many diversity initiatives in organizations, it is probably unconscious biases at the top that prevent faster progress. Whilst the diversity debate has run into a political dead-end, shouldn't it raise the question how leaders and teams at the top deal with information, thinking and approaches that are diverse, different or new? Aren't the best performing organizations those that can turn psychological diversity into innovative solutions and better business results? Would it be more productive to look at diversity as an issue of "open" versus "closed" organizations reflecting the open- or closed-mindedness of the top executives?

Schein (1985) refers to culture as "the feel of an organization". Instead of large-scale quantitative surveys of organizational cultures, he recommends using more subjective, qualitative methods, such as observations and interviews. Similarly, in *Breaking Through Culture Shock* (2001), I suggested looking at the architecture, atmosphere and service levels of airports more closely to get a first "feel" for a country, its society and culture.

What dimensions of business cultures should we consider? The following may be helpful:

▷ Power distance (hierarchy/structure)
▷ Long- and short-term perspective of companies
▷ Flexibility and tolerance of ambiguity
▷ Time- and schedule-planning (is it sequential from A to B to C, or synchronic doing different activities at the same time?).

Table 4.4 shows one way to explore business cultures, using the examples of Germany, the UK and China.

These are obviously stereotypical examples and not every company in Germany, the UK or China will show this pattern.

If we accept the juxtaposition of business cultures in Table 4.4, it may explain the strengths of high-technology products in Germany, of the creative industry in the UK, and the advantages of combining long-term planning with a good dose of pragmatism in many Chinese businesses. But which business culture is more adaptive?

Multiculturalism in Asia

Understanding Asian business cultures clearly takes more than looking at a snapshot of differences, as in Table 4.4. And as

Table 4.4 Differences in business cultures

Germany	UK	China
• hierarchical system • thorough approach • long-term perspective • sequential time-planning • separation between private and public life • low tolerance of ambiguity • less flexible system	• flatter structure • speed and flexible approach • short-term orientation • overlap between private and public life • high tolerance of ambiguity • flexible system	• hierarchical • short- and long-term orientation • pragmatic attitude • synchronic time-planning • overlap between private and public life • high tolerance of ambiguity • flexible business system

Shirish Apte pointed out, it is neither correct nor useful to use "Asia" as the big category that can subsume the many cultures of Asia. The example of Singapore illustrates this clearly.

Singaporeans were recently encouraged by their former leader Lee Kuan Yew, widely recognized as the founder of modern Singapore, to learn more about China in order to advance business relations between the two nations. Lee Kuan Yew urged Singaporeans

> ...to live in China for a long time in order to really understand Chinese culture and become truly bicultural...if we believe that because we speak Chinese, we understand the culture, that is wrong. We are Westernized, China is not Westernized. That makes a very big difference. For us, we follow the rule of law. For them, an agreement is the beginning of a long friendship, in which you make adjustments as you go along, considering what is fair (*The Straits Times*, 29 November 2012).

Lee Kuan Yew's view on biculturalism is clear: Singaporeans should live in China to become truly bicultural. In the same article, Lee Kuan Yew described how he learned about these business differences through initial misunderstandings in joint projects between the two countries, until Singapore eventually adjusted its approach to the Chinese way of doing business.

Are some organizations or organizational cultures more resilient and better able to adapt and perform in the current economic turmoil?

Resilience and Performance

In a business setting where the 1980s culture of "man as machine" has prevailed for too long, words like "resilience" are hardly ever used. Yet this was the theme for the 2013 World Economic Forum meeting in Davos: Resilient Dynamism, referring to the challenge of individuals, companies and countries to manage the current economic crisis. As the founder of the World Economic Forum, Klaus Schwab, writes: "to be resilient is to possess the ability to adapt to changing contexts, to withstand sudden shocks and to recover from them while still pursuing critical goals.... Either attribute – resilience or dynamism – alone is insufficient as leadership will require both."

Key aspects of resilience

As mentioned in Chapter 2, one chairman's response to the question how had his company's senior executives coped with the economic crisis was unexpected: predictions of who would perform well in the crisis were often wrong. And this experience was echoed by a number of other chairmen. Senior executives whom it was thought would be effective often failed and "undiscovered talent" came through and started to shine in the midst of volatility. Maybe the "undetected turnaround executives" did not have a chance to exercise their skills in a period of growth. But maybe the difference in performance is due to different levels of individual resilience.

Individual resilience

Individual resilience is "the flexibility in response to changing situational demands and the ability to bounce back from negative emotional experiences" (Tugdale et al, 2004). The self-management of emotions and the management of stress are essential to adapt to changing circumstances. Whether we experience negative emotions or stress depends on the interpretation of the situation as well as the evaluation of our resources and capability to deal with the situation.

Following Lazarus (1966), the *primary appraisal* of a situation determines whether we perceive the situation as threatening. The *secondary appraisal* involves the evaluation of one's resources to deal with the situation. Low resilience is typically found in individuals with negative and pessimistic appraisals and one of the most effective ways to increase resilience is to change negative expectations into more realistic or optimistic ones. Research on problem-solving has shown that negative emotions (such as fear or depression) limit the number and range of solutions we produce. Negative emotions also reduce our level of empathy with others and affect our interpersonal relationships.

The 2013 Davos program on Resilient Dynamism also focused on the health and resilience of individuals and one of the program highlights was Professor Mark Williams' seminar on "Mindfulness" or "Awareness". Originally applied in clinical psychology to alleviate stress and depression, mindfulness training has a much wider application, including the areas of education, leadership and creativity.

Williams' thesis is that mindfulness or awareness training builds resilience and increases flexibility, creativity and engagement. According to Professor Williams, who is the founder of Oxford University's Mindfulness Centre, the following comments describe typical behavior in the 21st Century: "It seems I am running on automatic, without much awareness of what I am doing" or "[I] find myself listening to someone with one ear, whilst doing something else at the same time".

As Williams explains, "we are in a 'doing-mode' most of the time. This is characterized by being on automatic pilot, taking all thoughts as real (even if they are highly self-critical and undermining), and then striving until we are exhausted and no longer functioning creatively."

The consequence of this "doing-mode" is that we miss important information and have so-called attentional blindness; we become rigid in our thinking, employing old habits of mind that solved a previous problem but are not suited to the current situation.

For most problems, all elements of a solution are already present but we cannot see them because of habits and conditioning, overgeneralization, fear and fatigue. Mindfulness or awareness training, primarily achieved by short meditation practices and other awareness exercises, helps to "re-set to zero", changing the prevailing mode of "doing" into "being" – shifting the self-focusing from conceptual to experiential. It is not just switching from action mode into reflection mode but using all our senses or awareness and not relying solely on the conceptual aspects of mind/brain that tend to prefer familiar patterns even after they have ceased to be effective or productive.

Mindfulness invites us to see clearly what is nourishing and what is depleting and it allows us therefore to energize or re-energize ourselves, one of the most important ways to build resilience (Williams, personal communication, 2013).

If we are not able to re-energize ourselves, we are certainly not able to energize others or a team – an essential factor for effective leadership.

Resilience in teams

Many change programs should start with the question: "How can I energize the team for the forthcoming changes or challenges?" Or in other words, what type of leader is able to build resilience? Is it the "androgynous leader" (see Chapter 1), combining masculine (task- and action-oriented) with feminine (relationship and nourishing) characteristics, who is most likely to succeed? One way of increasing team resilience is through building strong relationships within the group and through the social support of the team.

It is useful to reflect on the PM Leadership Theory advanced by Misumi (1985), which distinguishes two main functions in a group: goal/performance achievement (P) and the group/self-preservation (M). M Leadership aims at increasing interpersonal encouragement and support, while reducing conflict. Effectively, several decades on from Misumi's original research, we would probably describe this as the difference between task and people orientation. Both the P (task) and the M (people) function are essential in any leadership and are seen as interacting dimensions. Depending on the extent each dimension is expressed, we can differentiate between four basic types: PM, Pm, pM and pm.

Effects of leadership style on performance

Research studies have consistently shown the following rank order of effectiveness of these four leadership styles: PM, pM, Pm, pm. This empirically proven order of effectiveness is a strong support for the thesis of psychological androgyny, showing similar high focus on task (P) and people (M). Interestingly, a lower task orientation combined with very strong people orientation (pM) still produces higher results than a high task orientation with low people orientation (Pm). Positive effects of this leadership style have been shown in relation to long-term achievement, work motivation and turnover. What is your own leadership style in relation to P and M and how effective has it been with different types of employees? Misumi's research was originally conducted in Japan but subsequent studies have found similar findings in as diverse places as Britain, Hong Kong, the United States and India.

The interview with Neil Berkett, Chief Executive of Virgin Media, in this chapter will show how a CEO, who is seen as high on P and high on M, has successfully changed the business and achieved an impressive turnaround by applying both components of leadership.

The hypothesis I am proposing is that leaders who are high on M build resilience in their team and that leaders who are high on P and M can accelerate organizational performance whilst dealing with volatility and crisis situations – they are able to show and effect "Resilient Dynamism".

Whereas in a period of growth, the focus on the task will produce results, ongoing global volatility requires leaders, teams and organizations to increase their resilience and that of their organization.

Are Chinese Leaders More Resilient and Agile?

Professor Chang Weining, whose main research focuses on stress and mental health in Asia, has a unique insight into this question. As a Chinese–American who was brought up in Taiwan and came as a graduate student to the US, she taught at the University of Houston, before joining the National University of Singapore and Nanyang Technological University. She is an expert on cross-cultural psychology. When asked whether Chinese leaders are more resilient, her response was an unqualified "yes": "we have enough research that supports the hypothesis that the Chinese are more resilient than Westerners." There are various reasons for this stronger resilience. These include:

▷ **The view of the self**
According to Professor Chang, "Westerners or Americans have a belief in a 'stable self' or a 'principled self' as unyielding and not flexible. The Chinese, by contrast, see the self throughout life as *a process of development* – it is a dynamic process of evolution." The Asian view of self is steeped in Confucius – the message is to develop what is beneficial. Most Asians learn early on to change the things you can change and accept the things you cannot change. "Most Westerners look at Asian serenity as yielding and accommodating and think it is a sign of defeat and weakness, but it is in fact an adaptive process."

▷ **Illusion of control and adaptability**
"The West has an excessive illusion of control – to the extent that Westerners believe they can control things that are clearly uncontrollable. Asians may have an exaggerated sense of non-controllability. Their mantra is 'to work with the situation' and to accept the situation and look for opportunities – that is adaptability to circumstances." In the West, coming to that realization is seen as part of wisdom and maturity. But the Chinese are taught these lessons early on in schools and within families. For example, intellectual families teach Mandarin to their children through the reciting of classical texts and poetry, thereby instilling these views and Confucian philosophy. In China and throughout the world, "Confucius colleges" follow the same idea, exposing children to Chinese philosophy early on through the classics.

▷ **Response to volatility**
This focus on adaptability can act as a buffer against stress when faced with volatility and unpredictable events. The Chinese accept unpredictability and non-controllability of many situations as a rule. Chang supports her view that Chinese are more resilient than Westerners with research

on post-traumatic stress disorder (PTSD), defined as serious psychological symptoms in response to traumatic events. After 9/11, it was found that Asians (Asian Americans) had fewer symptoms of PTSD compared to their American (i.e. Caucasian) counterparts in New York. Similar cross-cultural differences were found when comparing the response to serious floods in Queensland (Australia) and in China. Six months after the floods, it was found that 16 percent of the population of Queensland suffered from PTSD symptoms, compared to 6 percent in the previously flooded province in China.

▷ **Management of emotions**
The Chinese notions of "self as a study in progress" and "the self as malleable" already have an in-built element of resilience, as "you learn to manage your emotions", according to Chang. Following the prevailing Buddhist and Taoist traditions, life is seen as transient and the Chinese learn early on that the world is bigger than you. Learning to manage your emotions, particularly in volatile situations, is one of the key factors in the increased resilience of the Chinese.

▷ **Situational attunedness – high level of external sensitivity**
The malleable self and the belief of interconnectedness, as well as being part of something bigger than oneself, prepare the Chinese early on to be highly sensitive towards their environment and changing circumstances. What we Westerners may see as a pragmatic attitude is likely a faster response to changing circumstances due to a heightened external sensitivity. This observation is also made by Jill Lee in her comments on Asian teams later in this chapter.

▷ **Flexibility of coping**
Chang's research on stress and coping in Asia prompted her to develop a coping model for Asia. Her work suggests that the Chinese show the following three core competencies for coping:
1. Sensitivity towards the environment: what does the environment call for?
2. Ongoing development of a big repertoire of coping responses: the drive to learn more competencies
3. Flexibility with the aim to achieve a person–situation fit: what is the fit that enables you to achieve your goal? Taking a long-term view of accommodation to achieve the goal.

Professor Chang believes that Chinese executives are particularly well placed to use the current economic uncertainty to find strategic investment opportunities. In fact, studies indicate that the Chinese have a higher preparedness to make risky investment decisions because they believe they can fall back on an extended family network in case of catastrophic outcomes.

Characteristics of Chinese Leadership and Teams

Jill Lee, CFO of ABB North Asia and China, is a Singaporean who previously worked for Siemens AG in Germany. She confirmed the strong resilience of the Chinese.

Pragmatism and adaptability

> The Chinese are very resilient regarding changes; they are also quick to react. They are able to understand and focus on immediate implications and do not spend a lot of consideration to discuss all dimensions.
>
> They also know very quickly what the customer wants and how to penetrate the market. They are pragmatic and risk-taking, focusing more on the bottom-line, where the market is and what the customer wants. They have a shorter time-horizon and adapt to the fast changing nature of business in China.
>
> This approach has advantages but it must be balanced against long-term sustainability requirements. The sheer size of the country clearly allows the Chinese to demonstrate their entrepreneurial ability. Many companies in China are increasing their focus to develop long-term strategic capabilities in their leadership teams.

International teams in Asia

> The teams in Chinese companies are still predominantly Chinese – there are still cultural issues when they try to integrate foreigners. Some of the challenges relate to language differences and some are due to the lack of diversity in the leadership team, which makes it difficult for foreign individuals to integrate as minority in a large company.

Within China, there is a clear shift. In the past, you had a lot of younger people trying to learn from the foreigners and wanting to emulate them. Now, there is growing confidence of the Chinese because of the successful economy and there is a stronger view that we have something to offer and that others can learn from us too. Many Chinese companies are also going abroad to expand their business. Due to their growing confidence and the career opportunities they believe they have in Chinese companies, many young Chinese executives also choose to join Chinese firms.

Talent issues

For those companies that are expanding abroad, there is concern to get enough leaders to manage their international business. There is also increasing demand for the ability of their people to handle volatility. In the past, it was more on managing growth and now there is also a need to drive growth amid volatility and complexity. This of course is a focus of all companies nowadays.

What are the observations on teams in other parts of Asia? The subsequent comments by a Singaporean executive show the differences in Asian teams. This senior executive in financial services was previously based in London and is now working in Singapore.

The old distinction between Western individualism and Asian collectivism is probably too simplistic. Asians are individualistic but their individualism is tempered or modified by the myriad of complex relationships (hierarchies, ties of kinship, friendships, obligations and who you have lunch with) which exist in any setting – from the family, to the village, to society at large.

Asian leadership is one of the clearest and best defined relationships within any Asian society. If you are the boss, you are expected to behave like the boss – you are expected to promote a culture of dependency so there is no question who pays for lunch. Asian leadership also promotes a certain cult of personality – quirks are allowed and almost always tolerated. You should also expect to be at the end of a paternalistic love/hate relationship over which you have very little control.

In a constantly changing society, a team is probably no more than a collection of temporary relationships. Not a lifetime commitment, more like a summer romance (and we know how these usually end) and, strangely enough, I think a team sometimes outlives its useful lifespan for all the wrong reasons. Inertia, weaknesses, glass ceiling may all extend the shelf life of an underperforming team.

Turning around Virgin Media: Neil Berkett

Neil Berkett joined NTL, Virgin Media's predecessor, as Chief Operating Officer in September 2005 and played a key role in driving the company's merger with Telewest, the subsequent acquisition of Virgin Mobile, and a rebranding of the combined companies' residential operation under the Virgin brand in 2007. He was appointed Chief Executive of Virgin Media in March 2008. He is also a Non-Executive Director of the Guardian Media Group and a Trustee for the NSPCC.

Neil's career spans a wide range of highly competitive customer-facing industries in different countries. A New Zealand national, his previous roles include: COO at Prudential Insurance Company, Head of Retail at St George Bank, Senior General Manager of the Australian division of Citibank, Chief Executive at East–West Airlines Australia and Financial Controller at ICL Australia.

On 6 February 2013, it was announced that US company Liberty Global had acquired Virgin Media in a deal that valued the UK firm at $23.3 bn. After completion of the take-over, Neil Berkett will leave the company he turned around with an estimated $65m of shares. His comment on the deal in the *Telegraph* was: "It shows that if you have the right innovation and approach to customers, you can create value, even in a difficult market."

Richard Branson, whose Virgin empire owns about 3 percent of Virgin Media, tweeted on the announcement: "Congratulations to Neil Berkett and the team at @VirginMedia. Great turnaround over 7 years…"

The following interview describes the turnaround journey of Virgin Media and the key lessons of the CEO and top team.

How did you build your top team?
I began to instill the "story of leadership". Great leaders should be able to do three things: attract great leaders, align to purpose, create great leaders.

Stage I: Attract great leaders – getting the team right
I inherited a team from NTL Telewest and Virgin and realized after a while that the best in each company was not the best for the combined

entity. It is a mistake to assume people could do the same role in the combined, much larger entity. When I was appointed as Acting CEO, I started afresh, and within 18 months replaced all but one of my top team. When you start getting one or two good people, you can make a big difference. I essentially recruited talent with long-term capabilities. Also, I started to look at talent in a more creative way. For example, I recruited someone into a strategy role who is now the COO. I was confident that we could create a great team if we could get the best people and give them clarity and focus.

To get a better grip of calibre, we used competency assessments and reviewed the profiles carefully as to what the company really needed in the next business phase. I also made a conscious decision to wait with an appointment in order to get it right. For example, we needed a strong CFO with experience in financially distressed organizations. To fill the gap until we found the right candidate, I convinced the Chairman of the Audit Committee to come in as a secondment. This gave us the sufficient breathing space to find the right CFO. The Chairman of The Audit Committee then left the board and became a member of the Executive Team and was there for nearly 12 months. If one cannot attract the right calibre, it is better to be creative and develop the breathing space to find it.

What behaviors were you looking for?
I am definitely looking for one common behavioral quality which is *tenacity*. At Virgin Media, I was looking for people who could deal with the risks and the "ups and downs" of a turnaround. The "ups and downs" we went through together really bonded us as a team.

What were the dynamics?
There are of course natural tensions in a team, particularly if one is looking for potential successors, which can create conflicts. You essentially end up brokering between individuals, but you have ideally other individuals in the team who can create a "glue" and are also brokers.

Stage II: Aligning leaders to purpose – developing the team
We started this alignment first with the senior team alone and, after two to three years, expanded the alignment process to the top 25 in the company. Stage II has worked very well, which is proven by our excellent retention of executive talent. We have not lost a single senior executive voluntarily in the last five years.

What were some of your personal challenges in bringing the team together?
One thing that I had noticed is that I am much more comfortable with ambiguity than anyone else in the team. I can cope with ambiguity in a structured way. For me, the strategy map gives the framework which

allows thoughts to develop and to find solutions; it allows for adaptation and modification if needed. In our turnaround journey, we had clear strategic cornerstones and these were: *network–brand–people*. The key business parameters in our business are relatively straightforward. The quality of networks is our key physical asset. So the question is, how do our assets create a competitive advantage? What comes from the assets? We need to ensure that connectivity is at the core of the business, and then come the applications and getting the customers to use more data as well as leading the way in convergence.

I kept the story relatively simple and saw our mission as "making our people happy, customers happy, and shareholders happy".

What were critical moments in this alignment?
We had a bit of a moment a couple of years ago to align the organization and decided to create a visual stimulus, which in fact is a rocket that illustrated the cornerstones of the business and is also congruent with our brand. The physical rocket we created is also used as the company screensaver, constantly reminding our employees of our cornerstones and mission. We have statistical data that show this worked well and improved employee engagement substantially, as they had clarity on our core cornerstones. For example, in 2010 our employee engagement scale was low; it was felt that the organization was lacking in strategy and confidence, but in 2013, we were in the top quartile of engagement and top quartile of high performance. This story has helped to rally people. Essentially, the rocket became a visual mechanism for aligning the organization. The rocket also is in alignment with our brand value of fun.

Stage III: Creating great leaders – achieving sustainable performance

As this was your first full CEO role, how would you describe your own development?
As a CEO, one goes through occasional periods of doubt. I had a wobble in 2010, when I was not sure what I was doing the role for and whether it was the right thing to stay longer term – particularly as I am not overly motivated by money. But then I reminded myself promptly that I was here to complete the leadership cycle and that part of this was also to create great leaders. Having an internal successor was important and part of the leadership cycle, so that the organization does not lose momentum and has sustainability. The CEO needs to actively build a legacy and leave the organization in a state where it can thrive without him. [This topic is further explored in Chapter 5.]

My philosophy is that sticking to the core will show how to expand. For example, we have expanded to the venture of Wi-Fi outside the home, with the London Underground contract. An initiative of "getting into the cities" has allowed us to develop business with councils and to sell to mobile operators. Similarly, we expanded into applications with the connected TV. It is clearly an "inside-out strategy", not an outside-in strategy that we have pursued. When I suggested that we should develop the venture with London Underground, many of my colleagues in the top team were originally skeptical and questioned whether we should put large resources into a venture where the results were very uncertain. But I had a hunch and an intuition that this project could lead to other things, which has proven to be right. In essence, our expansion and innovation is evolutionary rather than revolutionary. As we become more successful, we clearly also expect to take more risks.

What other steps did you take to create leaders and sustainable performance?
We shifted the original focus from the Group Executive Committee (the top team of six or seven) to the whole group of senior leaders, the top 25 in the company. This brought better long-term alignment and purpose in the organization and ensured the engagement and cultural shift.

You have been very successful in turning around this business. How would you describe your own leadership style?
I am told I have an unusual mix. I am highly analytical but have the ability to connect at individual and group levels well. As a CEO, I use my analytical skills less to solve the problem than to challenge. I motivate people individually and have a high interest in my team members as individuals. This creates a strong bond between me as a CEO and individual team members – it also results in a higher drive to perform and deal with the challenges.

What are your cultural observations of the team and what are the cultural characteristics?
We are long on analytics and structure and short on innovation. If I am critical, we are also short on emotional intelligence and we are trying to attract more women at the senior level. I would describe our culture as caring, informal, human and more fun than some other companies.

How do you build resilience in the team and in the organization?
In some ways it is part of the objective setting. I set unreasonable objectives but also manage the expectations with the board. I probably can be too demanding but will give the board a more realistic figure to achieve. I develop a quite challenging environment and want people to solve problems differently.

I have regular and structured communication with the team. We have a very clear structure as to how we meet as a team, for example, every Tuesday for three hours, and every six weeks we meet for one day to address issues of governance and macro topics. Once a month, we do a financial review.

What are the key challenges for you in terms of dynamics?
First, keeping fresh is hard. We have achieved a lot through ambitious plans but now I can detect a certain organizational fatigue. Second, we do not celebrate success as much as we should. I am personally always immediately on to the next thing as soon as we have achieved the milestone, but we should celebrate our success much more. Third, there is an issue associated with diversity.

We need to have more executives with strong emotional intelligence and with fresh perspectives who challenge the top team more. For example, to address this, I made a bold decision of bringing a less experienced, innovative executive on to the top table, which has worked very well. Every eight to twelve weeks we also bring the top 25 together – you can facilitate the alignment that way much better.

What are for you the signs of a well-functioning team?
I know that the team is well functioning when we have adaptive debates with everybody contributing. Ideally, we have a high level of inquiry and engagement as opposed to an advocacy-driven discussion.

This interview shows the ideal implementation of a governance framework, complemented by a philosophy of creating high-performance teams through a leadership style that recognizes and understands the individual needs of senior executives, whilst aligning everyone to the long-term success of the company. Looking at the recent events at Virgin Media, it looks like the rocket has gone off!

5 Talent Over Structure

Chapter 5 will focus on three issues to get the right leadership at the top.

▷ The need for a strategic selection of the CEO and the top team
▷ Focusing on talent over structures
▷ Getting the cultural fit right.

Strategic Selection of Chief Executives and Top Teams

The call for better predictions of executive success is never more prominent than in the selection of chief executives. With the average tenure of a CEO in Britain's largest companies getting shorter and shorter, one wonders about the longer term impact of any CEO. The average tenure of chief executives in Britain's FTSE 100 companies was 5.6 years in 1996, and this shortened to 4.8 in 2007. Additionally, with many high-profile exits of chief executives, it seems urgent to look at the selection process, and recommend what company boards should ideally consider when selecting a new chief executive or key figures of their executive teams.

The introduction to this topic in Chapter 2 already suggested applying more sophisticated assessments that take account of the strategic goals and the culture of the organization, building on Miles and Snow's (1978) Typology of *prospectors, defenders* and *analyzers*.

Right now and in future, we probably need more and more organizations of the hybrid kind. A functional background analysis alone is not sufficient in establishing the fit with the strategic intent of the company, but as Hambrick (2001) demonstrated, a more in-depth understanding of leadership characteristics of the top management team (TMT) is needed. Hambrick and Mason (1984) argued:

▷ The organization is a reflection of its executives. "If we want to understand why organizations do the things they do, and why they perform the way they do, we must understand the experiences, values, motives and biases of the top executives" (Hambrick, 2001, p.38)
▷ The characteristics of the TMT matter more than the CEO's alone
▷ Demographic characteristics are a shortcut to understanding executives' psychology or preferences. Executives' experiences and personalities will influence the interpretation of business situations and affect their strategic decisions. In other words, we need to open the "black box" between demographics of executives and strategic choice and company performance. Hambrick and Mason's Upper Echelon Theory inspired a vast number of studies that demonstrated the effect of TMT characteristics on company performance. For example, Olsen, Parayitam and Twigg (2006) demonstrated significant relationships between demographic variables and strategic choice and company performance. In their sample of 66 firms in the telecommunication sector, they found a positive relationship between the TMT's functional heterogeneity and mergers and acquisitions, as well as internal innovation. TMT characteristics also have impact on a company's internationalization. In a study of 112 internationally diversified US-based firms in the manufacturing sector, Herrmann and Datta (2005) found that firms with higher levels of international diversification had TMTs with a higher educational level, shorter organizational tenures and younger executives. These TMTs also had greater international experience.

Before considering ways to assess the top team, let's look at the area that is highly researched and that has been given a lot of attention: the selection of chief executives.

Boards of troubled organizations have become impatient with their chief executives. But, surprisingly, the board is often caught off-guard in these situations, with little succession planning and no immediate successor to step in. Contrary to what we may expect from the more short-term-oriented US culture, American companies seem to be better at succession planning. British companies show a much lower rate of internally appointed CEOs (66 percent) compared to the USA (86 percent) (Marx 2008). Does succession planning in Britain simply lag behind the USA and is it less systematic, or does the UK generally favor external candidates? The same study also found that CEOs of the UK's Most Admired Companies are more likely to be internally appointed (86 percent) – strong succession management is shown in companies such as GlaxoSmithKline, Rolls-Royce, Diageo and Tesco.

Internal successors have a clear advantage over external contenders, as the risk of cultural misfit is reduced and their performance as a "known entity" is more predictable. But what board practices do we currently see in CEO selection from an executive search perspective?

In my experience, the best boards around the world currently implement the following practices:

▷ Effective succession planning starts with the CEO facing up to the eventuality of his/her own "executive exit" and planning it well in advance as part of legacy management. General Electric is always cited as the prime example of good succession planning: Jack Welch groomed three successors, with Jeff Immelt gaining the top role.

The best boards review and benchmark the executive group early on against the external market. This allows a better understanding of strengths and weaknesses and the planning of tailored development programs. For example, a private international company identified a potential successor years before the CEO's retirement. After an external evaluation of his leadership potential, he was systematically developed through international assignments in different regions, building an overseas operation and the restructuring of a business. He was also mentored at the time. It was an excellent example of what a well-planned development program could look like. Sometimes, this may be complemented by an external coach or by targeted business school programs.

▷ Large international companies take a much broader approach to succession planning and benchmark and develop their top 100 or 200 executives to keep atop the question, do we have the right leadership to execute the strategy?

▷ In case of a sudden CEO exit, the board ideally reviews the strategic success criteria for the future and benchmarks against the best international candidates available. Internal candidates should ideally be benchmarked against outside candidates. In the case that the internal candidate is appointed, this will give confidence to the board and external market.

▷ As we saw in Chapter 2, a CEO's success is likely determined in the ratio 30 percent technical skills, 30 percent personal attributes and 40 percent fit with the organizational culture. Nevertheless, most assessments primarily focus on technical skills, leaving the major part of a candidate's success factors unknown. The lack of cultural fit and fit with strategy is often the main reason why some CEOs perform very well in one company but fail in the next one. Getting this fit right requires more sophisticated procedures to answer the three essential questions outlined in Chapter 2:

1. Does the executive know how to create value in the situation in which they are recruited for? Does he/she have the right business competencies, prior experience, global understanding?
2. How will the person create value? What are his/her leadership characteristics, including drive, energy, resilience and values?
3. What is his/her fit with the organizational culture, the top team and the board, and in particular the Chairman?

This may be a good catalogue of questions for boards to ask.

CEO Success Factors

Research of 300 CEO transitions at S&P companies suggests that insiders are best in terms of long-term company performance when the company is doing well, whereas external candidates do better when the company is in trouble (Citrin and Ogden, 2010). The best performing CEOs in the same study were those who were board members and stepped in as CEO. The worst performing CEOs were those who were recruited as outsiders into other roles, like COO, before their appointment as CEO. Interestingly, this is a strategy that many companies still pursue if they have not groomed a successor.

One of the most significant global studies on best-performing CEOs (Hansen and Ibarra, 2010) analyzed the long-term performance and shareholder value of 2000 CEOs worldwide, including many in the emerging markets. The study considered CEOs who had started their role between 1995 and 2007 and ranked their long-term performance combining three measures: country-adjusted return, industry-adjusted return and change in market capitalization during tenure. The top five CEOs were:

▷ Steve Jobs, Apple
▷ Yun Jong-Yong, Samsung Electronics
▷ Alexey Miller, Gazprom
▷ John Chambers, Cisco Systems
▷ Mukesh Ambani, Reliance Industries.

Whilst many of the top performing CEOs are based in the US, strong performances are spread globally across 16 countries in the top 50 list and 25 countries in the top 200 list. Hansen and Ibarra (2010) commented on their findings: "the top 50 list shows no country or industry has a corner on performance. But taking a larger perspective did bring to light a number of hidden gems – quiet Chief Executives who delivered outstanding results year in and year out, away from the glare of the cover stories and business school case studies" (p.11, reprint).

In the context of CEO succession planning, it is important for boards to keep in mind the following factors that, according to the research of Hansen and Ibarra, seem to heighten the CEO's performance.

▷ Being an insider – although troubled companies in this study were more tempted to recruit an outsider
▷ Having an MBA: CEOs with an MBA ranked overall better
▷ Taking over troubled companies: against expectations, CEOs who took over poorly performing companies were more

successful than CEOs who took over companies that performed well previously.

The last finding is particularly encouraging in the current crisis. Could our views of CEO performance change significantly in the next ten years as a consequence of the current volatility and the need for leaders to navigate this uncertainty? Key questions for boards to ask relate to adaptability, diversity of experience and ambidextrous leadership skills. One of the areas for boards to explore with CEO candidates is whether they have shown success in different environments, including growth, restructuring, international operations, different sectors and different organizational cultures.

Recent research by Antoinette Schoar of MIT's Sloan Business School (*Financial Times*, 11 March 2012) suggests it may not be that easy to find CEO candidates who have these ambidextrous capabilities. Investigating whether the economic conditions at the start of a CEO's career have an effect on the way they later operate, Schoar found a clear "conditioning effect": if the CEO started in a downturn, he/she was more likely to be a cost-cutter throughout their career, independent of the specific business situation; and a similar pattern emerged in CEOs who started their career in a growth phase. These findings do not bear too well with regard to ambidextrous skills. Very few CEOs may have this capability – which is why boards need to extend their review from the CEO to the entire top team.

Executive Team Review

How does a CEO or leader of a business division know what they have got at the top? How does the company board know if the TMT has the right skills, attitudes and motivation to execute the company's strategy? In the past, this assessment was done intuitively but nowadays companies use an independent and detailed review, sometimes still called a "management audit". Traditionally, team audits comprised competency assessments through structured interviews by executive search consultants or other assessment specialists. Nowadays, and this is different from country to country, they are often complemented by psychological assessments of personality, values and motivation. The combination of competency-based reviews and psychological evaluations allows the business head to answer whether the team has the right skill set and also:

▷ How will the team apply these skills? What are its preferred styles and in what business situations will it be particularly successful? In turn, in what type of situations will it not succeed and should be complemented by other executives? Also, following the recommendations of positive psychology, how can the strengths of the team be better utilized in future?
▷ For international companies, does the team's experience and understanding reflect the international markets the company covers or is trying to grow? Does the team have sufficient diversity of cultural, functional or cognitive nature?

Executive Team Reviews are normally triggered by a change in strategy: the company wants to accelerate growth, needs a turnaround, or is planning a major acquisition and needs to understand if the current team is able to integrate the acquisition and operate at a larger, more complex level. Case 5.1 is an example of how an executive review was used to build the right team and platform for growth in an internationally operating company.

Case 5.1: Developing a Platform for Growth and Innovation

Case 5.1

A small financial services firm, founded by several partners, had built an excellent reputation with international clients. With international offices that spread from the US to the emerging markets, it was poised for substantial growth. The strategy was to double the size of the firm and grow the international side. The CEO wanted advice on the right organizational structure, and approached me for guidance. He wanted to achieve three things:

1. Ensure long-term sustainability of growth and effectiveness with which the firm was run

> 2. Give confidence to the investors regarding the success of the firm by introducing a more corporate structure (comparable to other financial services firms)
> 3. Design a structure that would leave room for innovation.
>
> It sounded an interesting project and I liked the reputation of the firm. The briefing with the CEO went in a fairly predictable way: an analysis of the current state and future strategy of the organization, a look at its history, what worked and did not work, how aligned the team was regarding structural ideas and the desired outcome of the project.
>
> The briefing was quite extensive and so it was only in the last ten minutes that we explored the present organizational culture and the composition and dynamics of the top team. In fact, the last ten minutes made it clear that the primary issue was not the organizational structure at all but having the right talent at the top: the right people in the right roles, who were able to create the best culture for the future growth of the organization. The organizational structure was secondary. Moreover, the CEO explained that the nine executives of his top team were all essential for the future of the company and were not "replaceable". But were their current roles right for the future, or should they take additional or different responsibilities? Indeed, would they choose to stay? What were their short- and longer term career aims?

The project of designing the right organizational structure for this fast-growth financial services firm quickly turned into an Executive Team Review, with a developmental angle and an analysis of the aspirations of the senior executives. We decided to also look at the team dynamics, as the team seemed to have a wide range of views on how to build the platform for growth.

Executive Development Reviews and Team Review

The project comprised the following elements:

1. *Individual Development Reviews*, including discussions on career aspirations, team dynamics and culture of the firm.

The Executive Review consisted of a three-hour competency-based interview. Examples of competencies were:

- Strategic ability
- Entrepreneurial orientation
- Process skills and operational effectiveness
- Market awareness
- Innovation and product development
- International orientation and understanding
- Team skills
- Motivation and ambition.

Interviews focused on executives' past experiences in these areas. The approach has high face validity and typically generates a high level of engagement and buy-in. Many executives actually enjoy the process, as it gives them an opportunity to reflect on their careers in great detail. Subsequent reports are competency related, and executives can easily understand the findings and plan action steps to address any development areas.
2. *Team review questionnaire*
3. *Individual confidential reports*
    These are discussed in the feedback sessions, with particular focus on the individual's strengths in contributing to the growth of the company, on recommendations to address the individual's development needs and on how career aspirations can be realized in the next stage of the firm.
4. *Strategic summary of all executive reviews in a team profile*
5. *Feedback of the strategic results to the CEO and Chairman.* This involved discussions on organizational recommendations, including structure and the development of the team.
6. *CEO feedback session with each executive* to ensure internal follow-up and clarification of next roles. This follow-up guarantees that recommendations are immediately implemented in the organization and that the firm gains maximum benefits from the Executive Review. The follow-up sessions also helped the CEO to engage more closely with his team and to gain the psychological buy-in to the next phase of the business.

Key findings

In relation to the planned growth, the following emerged:

▷ To answer the big question many boards and CEOs have, the bench strength of this TMT against the external market was very good; the group of executives scored highly throughout. This very much spoke for the recruitment the firm had done in the past; it was able to attract the right talent. The results indicated, however, that not everyone was in the right role and the team had great competencies that were underutilized.

▷ Despite the high calibre of the team, it was "lopsided"; it was exceptionally strong on the intellectual side (analytical thinking, innovation and creativity) but weak on processes and people, i.e. it was ineffective in putting structures, processes, metrics in place, and in leadership and talent development. This imbalance threatened the growth strategy: the top team was good at developing ideas but lacked implementation and leadership capabilities.

This imbalance needed addressing if the firm wanted to grow. Moreover, this result confirmed that the organizational structure is pretty irrelevant if you do not have the right competencies across the board, i.e. if you do not have the right people in the right roles to implement the strategy. Organizational structures often give an "illusion of control", as they are tangible and overt and are perceived as "change is happening" in the company.

It is perfectly understandable that most TMTs and boards give substantial attention to the structure and resulting roles and accountabilities in the organization. It is an important way to have control. Nevertheless, with the top team, it is useful to look at talent first, and apply an interative process of structure, roles and talent, as this is the best way to utilize strengths and counterbalance weaknesses, as well as taking into account the personal aspiration of executives. In the present market, many CEOs ask whether their team has the agility to adapt to a fast-changing world and how the team skills can be more flexibly used instead of sticking rigidly to roles.

▷ The competency review showed that the team had two factions – an entrepreneurial contrasting a corporate one. It illustrated the challenge to create a more corporate platform whilst keeping an entrepreneurial and innovative spirit. It suggested a "light" corporate structure.

▷ Some executives were not in the right roles; some innovative, market-oriented executives were in operationally focused roles. Their roles needed to be changed, and executives with stronger operational skills needed to be recruited.
▷ A better understanding of individual career ambitions helped to redefine several roles, and a comparison with organizational structures of other financial services companies showed gaps and resulted in several additional roles.

Executives were explicit about the dichotomy of the current culture. The firm was fragmented and described as:

▷ Innovative versus process
▷ Free thinking versus corporate
▷ Content oriented versus reward oriented.

Team Dynamics

Whilst the CEO was highly rated, team effectiveness was rated as relatively low. The team lacked transparency in decision-making; it did not have a clear strategy and lacked performance management. The team had "stalled". Despite this, the atmosphere in the top team and the firm was still very positive. What emerged was rather a lack of discipline and performance orientation, quite typical of an organization in transition.

The review of roles and dynamics led to a pragmatic approach for the team to address its structure and governance. The benefits of the approach were threefold:

▷ Most executives obtained more desirable roles as a consequence of this project
▷ The intervention energized the top team to start the next phase of growth
▷ The new structure accelerated the growth of the company.

Chief executives will benefit from a more sophisticated understanding of the interplay between executive profiles, the strategy of the firm and organizational performance. Professor Andrew Pettigrew, of Oxford's Saïd Business School, suggests that it is understanding the "black box", the social interactions and dynamics that are going on in the top team and on the board, that will make a difference.

To access the "black box" further, complementing the competency assessment with psychological evaluation (personality profile or values assessment), will not only allow a better understanding of leadership style but will enhance the predictability of success and risks of a team.

A Differentiated View of Business Skills, Leadership Style and Motivational Drivers

The following case examples show what a more differentiated review of executives can deliver in different company scenarios.

Succession management

Case Example 5.1

A succession management project with the top 15 executives of a large international company indicated that the skill sets at the top were well aligned with the strategic goals of the company. However, the overall skill set was too homogeneous. This can be a risk to long-term success. If the business model changes or a competitor is much more innovative, the company is not prepared to adapt. Moreover, the international capabilities of the senior group was not "in sync" with its plans for further expansion; only a few executives had had long international assignments and the level of cross-cultural understanding was at best "average". The personality analysis showed the group was not very comfortable with ambiguity and uncertainty and was slightly risk-averse.

Private-equity-based business

Case Example 5.2

A private-equity backed UK-based technology company merged with a Continental European company. The private equity company wanted clarification on the following issues:

▷ What is the ideal structure of the merged business?

▷ Looking at the executives in the two companies, who should have what role?
▷ What were the cultural differences between the two companies?
▷ What were the key steps for a faster integration and an acceleration of the performance of the top team?

The evaluation methodology in this case was heavily oriented towards a psychological one in order to gain a better understanding of the operating leadership styles in the two companies. The objective was to combine the best features of the two firms in the merged organization. The findings reversed some of the previous role decisions; for example, the CEO of the Continental company was originally earmarked as the future Chairman but the assessment showed he was much too "hands-on" for a chairman role and was, therefore, appointed Chief Executive of the merged company.

International expansion

Case Example 5.3

To succeed in its international expansion, a private company started systematic leadership development of its nine most senior executives worldwide. Executives in this organization had a long tenure and their skill sets and leadership style were well known. The company knew its executives' skills were well aligned with the goals of the business and the business was very successful in its sector. Nevertheless, the CEO wanted clarification on two pressing questions. Firstly, how does the senior team benchmark against international standards? A question any company with long-tenured executives should ask periodically, especially if the competition gets stronger. Secondly, are there any additional skills in the team that could bring more innovation? And how prepared and agile was the team with regard to the internationalization agenda? The results of this development project were interesting:

▷ The team benchmarked well against the external market
▷ It showed a good combination of problem-solving skills and execution and a balance between strategic and operational effectiveness

▷ The team was weak on leadership skills and did not empower others. This impacted the business performance these executives could achieve with their teams, and led to leadership development for some individuals
▷ The senior group was more innovative than previously assumed. Therefore, the CEO started to review how this innovation could be used more effectively
▷ The international capability varied widely. The psychological profile showed that the team was "quite set" and not particularly flexible, and that closer cross-regional collaboration and more discussion of global issues would help to develop the team further. Becoming more flexible and adapting to ambiguity was one of the themes that the CEO subsequently addressed. Several executives obtained some external coaching and the results informed future recruitment criteria.

Career development and retention of the top team

Case Example 5.4

A different objective was pursued by a CEO of a knowledge-based company. This CEO had successfully run the business for six years and had an excellent, close-knit team. He did not have any concerns about the skill set or effectiveness of the top team; his main concern was their long-term retention and their "role enrichment". Some executives had been with the firm for a long time and were hard to replace. The CEO wanted to understand whether he could enlarge/enrich the roles of his executive team. A psychological development approach was taken, focusing on career ambition, motivation and life goals. Each executive had several development/coaching sessions as part of this project. The CEO followed up with "calibrated" and productive career discussions with each executive. The executives were much clearer about how they could use their skill sets and realize their ambitions in the next phase of the company.

Assessment Methods

As the above case examples show, there are a variety of methodologies and approaches that can improve the team–strategy–fit and the understanding of how teams create value for the company. Assessment methods include:

▷ competency-based interviews
▷ psychological evaluation
▷ 360° feedback (quantitative or qualitative)

The choice of methodology depends on the objectives and factors to be assessed.

Objective	Methodology
• selection	• competency-based interviews
• selection plus fit and development	• competency-based interviews plus psychological assessment
• development	• psychological assessment and/or 360° feedback

Global leadership competencies

Most organizations have their own competency frameworks to evaluate and promote their executives. "Global competence" is not always listed as a key competence – potentially assuming that most of us are internationally versatile. But as we know from failures in teams and in international mergers, the significance of international competence is often underrated.

As shown in Chapter 2, the assessment of business competencies was originally promoted by executive search companies through their "management audits". Business competencies are assessed in structured interviews and on the basis of past experience. Search consultants are well versed in calibrating executives: if you are interviewing hundreds of senior executives every year, you are able to benchmark well.

The effectiveness of competency assessments depends on several factors:

▷ The right framework of competencies
▷ Consistency of competency evaluation and scoring
▷ A "contextual" interpretation of results
▷ Sensitive but clear feedback to the executive and a productive follow-up in the organization.

Consistency of scoring is achieved by a detailed scoring system, allowing the translation of qualitative interview responses into quantitative scores; scores can range from "1 to 5" or from "1 to 7". This also allows a team profile of aggregated scores to be produced, which can be very useful. For example, the competency profile of a team may show that the team is extremely effective in developing customer relationships and can produce strong results through its high operational effectiveness. However, it may simply stick with well-proven solutions, even when the environment changes, due to a lack of innovation and strategic thinking at the top.

Apart from overall scores, the variance in each dimension gives essential information about the different levels of the respective competence in the team and the homogeneity or heterogeneity of the team. For example, whilst the team may be low in innovative abilities, there may be an executive who scores exceptionally high in this field and so an innovation hub could be built around him/her, comprised of similarly creative executives at different levels of the company. Ideally, we also want a more "balanced" view on how the existing strengths of the team can be more effectively applied in future.

Individual reports focus very much on the qualitative content and a nuanced interpretation of the competencies, ensuring an effective situational interpretation of the results. This approach has high face validity as the relevance of the process can immediately be understood and executives often enjoy discussing their experience in a more structured way.

An assessment of business competencies is crucial in many scenarios but it is not explicit regarding questions of "cultural fit" or the way the executive applies the competencies and the motivation to do so. These are psychological questions and require a different approach. A combination of competency *and* psychological evaluation provides a more differentiated view of individuals and teams.

Psychological assessments

Chapter 3 outlined some of the psychological characteristics of effective international executives, following the Culture Shock Triangle of global leadership.

There is certainly one personality type that should raise concerns in global business – the *Type A* executive, showing impatience and aggressiveness, tenseness, a "time is money" attitude, combined with the desire for control, poor listening and the preference for fast actions. This is the stereotypical 1980s Wall Street banker. This "role model" has been replaced by the globally effective executive who is able to build long-term business relationships rather than competitively beating everyone they meet. The "trader model" has been superseded by the "relationship builder".

Psychological assessments usually follow the format of a half-day and sometimes even one-day assessment, comprising of:

▷ Psychological interview
▷ Series of personality questionnaires
▷ Analysis of career values
▷ Feedback of results and analysis regarding future roles, international capabilities, and fit with strategy and organization.

Development areas are discussed in relation to the Culture Shock Triangle of emotions, thinking and behavior, explaining how the different personality attributes can affect business performance and results. Psychological assessments are frequently used in the UK and many organizations have an in-house assessment capability. Companies are typically more interested in using in-depth assessments after high-profile failures in senior appointments at the top.

Whereas in the past, we found distinct cross-cultural differences in the acceptability of assessments, this has changed in the last couple of years. There is an increased demand all over Asia and South America for assessments in selection and development situations. Within the UK, using in-depth psychological evaluations up to CEO level is well accepted. This is less common in Germany or France. Cultures with a strong divide between work and personal life may be more reluctant to introduce psychological assessments at very senior levels.

Assessment of Foreign Nationals

Interviewers often make up their mind about an interviewee within 30 seconds of meeting them. It suggests we are "ruled" by unconscious and conscious biases, where non-verbal signals and appearance can determine the success of an interview. Research has shown that the taller US presidential candidate wins the election, attractive executives attain higher salaries and candidates with foreign names are deselected in written applications.

Unconscious biases

Whereas some of the conscious biases have been addressed by effective legislation, "unconscious biases" are more difficult "to tackle" – after all, they are "not conscious". One of the most common biases is the *"halo effect"*, whereby one projects one positive characteristic, such as being tall, on to all the other and often less observable characteristics, such as intelligence. Another common bias, and a universal one, is that we like and select people "who are like us". We like to spend time with people who have similar interests, attitudes and often underlying personality characteristics. "Recruiting in one's own image" is evident in many situations but has been particularly criticized in the contentious discussion on boardroom diversity with regard to the "snail-like pace" of women's progression to boards (see Chapter 6 on this topic).

Biases, conscious and unconscious, are part of human nature, and they may be particularly evident when evaluating people from "other" cultures. In order to make sense of the world, and the thousands of stimuli and bits of information we are confronted with, we apply "categories" or "lenses" through which we see the world; this happens in the interpretation of business situations, the interpretation of executives' behavior and of their calibre. And often the less familiar the signals are, the stronger our lenses react – the less differentiated and more stereotypical our conclusions become. And sometimes, a business leader is simply not able to form a final opinion on a candidate and needs additional information, as in the following scenario.

Case Example 5.5

A successful CEO of a British-based company with operations around the world interviewed an American candidate for a position

5 ▶ TALENT OVER STRUCTURE

> in his management team in New York. The CEO interviewed the candidate and had the following reaction: "The candidate has the perfect skill set and was incredibly impressive in the interview. He presented well, he was easy to strike rapport with, and he had a positive attitude. Yet, I did not understand him or his motivation for the role. In fact, the candidate presented himself in such a positive way, that I cannot decide whether I have found 'Superman', whether this is just a cultural difference in presentation style, or whether the candidate simply followed a smooth script that was meant to cover up the weaknesses, or even serious flaws. I need more information and ideally a full psychological evaluation to understand the candidate better."

As we saw in Chapter 4, cultures differ in communication styles and the way executives present themselves, are evaluated and promoted. We all benefit from reflecting on how we respond to individuals who have very different backgrounds. The most obvious situation is when we evaluate executives who work in a non-native language. As Thomas Geitner pointed out, it is generally acknowledged that you tie up 30 percent of your intelligence for communication when initially working in a foreign language.

Some methods that can be used to combat our biases include introducing more objectivity and independent views into selection decisions and using more objective measures, such as psychological assessments.

Cross-cultural assessments

The best psychological tests and questionnaires are well researched, with good validity and reliability coefficients. But even the best tests do not allow a perfect prediction of ability or personality characteristics – the psyche is simply not perfectly metric! Also, the value of psychometrics very much depends on the context in which they are used; for example, they require a positive engagement of candidates which can vary, depending on the cultural acceptability of assessments or the familiarity with the process. Although psychometrics were designed to bring a scientific and more objective basis to assessments, their value is only as good as the quality of interpretation by the assessors – essentially, there is a great deal of art in the interpretation of science. And the interpretation is particularly challenging when assessing foreign nationals or in, as psychologists call it, cross-cultural testing.

Essentially, no test is fair to all cultures – tests usually favor the culture that developed it. So, what should organizations and executives be aware of in international assessment scenarios? In his influential article on cross-cultural assessment, Lonner (1990) suggested checking the following:

1. *Familiarity of testing or assessments for the specific cultural or ethnic group*
   Are assessments the norm, as in many Western companies nowadays? Or are they relatively new, as in some of the emerging markets? If they are new, more careful introductions and explanations of the process and how the results are used are warranted.
2. *The universality of the concept/construct to be assessed*
   As Lonner pointed out, if we take our Western concept of intelligence as being smart, fast and relatively narrowly defined in terms of analytic or academic intelligence and contrast it with how intelligence may be defined in some African cultures, i.e. "slow" in terms of thoughtfulness and wisdom, this comparison shows the complexity of applying the same interpretation of results irrespective of the cultural background of the person assessed.
3. *Replacing verbal with non-verbal stimuli does not make the test culture free*
   Attempts to reduce the cultural bias by using non-verbal stimuli showed that, strictly speaking, all stimuli are "culturally loaded" and therefore favor individuals from the culture in which the methodology was originally developed.

Particularly in ability tests with time limits, the effects of working in a non-native language need to be taken into account and statistical corrections applied to the final score. Even in fully bilingual executives, there is typically a dominant language and we cannot expect the same reading speed in the non-dominant language. In selection interviews, it is easy to underestimate cultural differences in behavior and presentation style, especially if the candidate is an international executive with excellent business English. Some cultural differences are particularly evident in 360° feedback scenarios.

360° feedback

As part of the development of their senior talent, most organizations use annual feedback from immediate work colleagues. The feedback results can also have an impact on the bonus element of the executives' remuneration. These types of 360° reviews are typically computerized and dimensions are assessed on a "1 to 5" scale. The executive also completes a self-assessment. Results are interpreted in relation to several factors:

▷ How close are self- and other ratings? In other words, how does the person's view of him/herself tally with the views of others?
▷ Are there big differences between the scores of subordinates, peers and superiors?
▷ What development areas should be addressed and are there strengths that could be used more widely?

The value of the 360° feedback depends on the accuracy and openness of assessors and an individual's level of self-reflection and openness when self-assessing.

The way we lead and the impact we create are also discussed at board level. At a development review of the executive group in an international company I have worked with, the non-executive board directors focused very much on the leadership style of each executive, i.e. *how* they led and *what* they created in the organization. Business schools use 360° feedback in their leadership modules as a major tool for self-development. Business academics view continuous learning as a core "meta competency" of a leader and continuous learning on leadership is part of this.

At INSEAD's Leadership Module, we work very effectively with an in-depth, 360° feedback methodology, the Global Executive Leadership Inventory (GELI) developed by Professor

Manfred Kets de Vries. This well-constructed instrument assesses 12 dimensions of global leadership:

▷ Visioning
▷ Empowering
▷ Energizing
▷ Designing and Aligning
▷ Reward and Feedback
▷ Team Building
▷ Outside Orientation
▷ Global Mindset
▷ Tenacity
▷ Emotional Intelligence
▷ Life Balance
▷ Resilience to Stress.

Often, we find that executives have relatively low stress resilience and insufficient life balance – and this is not just a pattern in executive MBAs or mid-level executives but also applies to very senior levels. As outlined before, the data on executives' resilience from a variety of sources suggests focusing more on this area in order to increase individuals' resilience.

Moreover, as a person's stress resilience is virtually impossible to assess by observation only (hence the gap between self-reported low resilience and a higher resilience rating by others), low resilience may be undetected by others for a long time but affect the executive's performance and decision-making ability.

Strengths-based Assessment

Psychology has historically been "deficit oriented" – diagnosing weaknesses and creating development programs to address these. But with the advance of positive psychology, the picture has changed. Positive psychology focuses on wellbeing, creativity and happiness. It focuses on personal and professional strengths. As Hefferon and Boniwell (2011) suggest, using our strengths can build psychological resilience. Positive psychology recommends a strengths-based approach rather than fixating on weaknesses.

I have always argued for a more creative definition of executives' roles around talent rather than fitting them in to a narrow

5 ▶ TALENT OVER STRUCTURE

job description. Admittedly, this may be more feasible in entrepreneurial organizations than in corporate ones. Focusing on strengths increases optimism and confidence and re-energizes – positive effects that are urgently needed in today's pressurized environment. Hefferon and Boniwell cite that employees using their strengths are significantly more engaged than those who do not use their strengths.

Using one's strengths can also get us to the highest form of engagement – into "flow". "Also, and importantly, within sport and occupational domains, is the concept of group flow where people report being in flow in tandem with their fellow teammates" (Hefferon and Boniwell, 2011, p.82). This is what typically happens in high-performance teams when team members are "in tune with each other" – when they take a personal interest in each other's success and wellbeing. These teams generate positive emotions and achieve much higher performance.

Fredrickson and Losada's (2005) interesting research shows the ideal ratio of positive to negative emotions in flourishing business teams. Studying high- and low-performance teams in terms of their quality of interaction (positive versus negative), whether they asked questions or told (enquiry versus advocacy) and whether they talked about themselves or others (self- or others centred), they found clearly differentiating factors of high-performance teams: higher positive to negative interaction (6 to 1), more enquiry and discussions that focus on others rather than themselves – a pattern that suggests a completely different level of engagement compared to low-performance teams.

The task of a leader is to bring optimism, confidence and hope to the organization. Managing the emotions of the team is a key area for any team leader. Our mood affects the quality of problem-solving and positive mood is correlated with higher creativity. Our mood also affects the quality of solutions to interpersonal problems. People in a positive mood are able to find effective solutions to interpersonal problems, in contrast to people in a negative mood who seem stuck.

In cross-cultural encounters, it has been shown that people with higher levels of positive emotions take a broader perspective and show greater feelings of sympathy. When we are experiencing positive emotions, we are better at recognizing others' viewpoints and, therefore, develop stronger relationships with others.

The management of emotions is essential in building resilience. Resilience is seen by some researchers as having two components: the flexibility to adapt to changing situational requirements and the ability to recover fast from emotional setbacks. Experience in managing culture shock in international work can also build resilience. As we saw in Chapter 2, international executives who have lived and worked abroad for a minimum of one year see themselves as having higher self-confidence, better strategic abilities and more effective communication skills as a direct result of their expatriate experience (Marx, 1996).

Effective team leadership means being aware and managing the emotional turbulence in a team. Following the recommendations of positive psychology, a CEO may significantly increase the resilience of a team and an organization by using a strengths-based approach.

The Innovator's DNA

Professor Hal Gregersen at INSEAD has spent considerable time analyzing what makes organizations innovative and how we can assess the innovation potential of individuals and teams. Over a period of six years, he and his co-authors studied the behavior of 25 innovative entrepreneurs and surveyed more than 3000 executives and 500 individuals who had started companies and invented products that were highly innovative (Dyer, Gregersen and Christensen, 2009). Importantly, and as the interview with Rory Sutherland in Chapter 3 showed, senior executives of the most innovative companies do not delegate creative work; they do it themselves. In less innovative companies, top executives delegate the work if they see themselves responsible for facilitating the *process* of innovation but not for innovation itself.

The most creative executives differ from less creative ones in five critical dimensions – the five criteria of the Innovator's DNA (Dyer et al, 2009):

1. *Associating*
   Central to innovation is the ability to connect diverse and seemingly unrelated ideas and experiences from different fields. This is similar to Daniel Pink's thesis in his book *A Whole*

New Mind and to Steve Jobs' experiences, for example, using his early calligraphy classes to develop the iconic typeface for Apple's computer programs. As the researchers summarize: "the world's most innovative companies prosper by capitalizing on the divergent associations of their founders, executives, and employees" (Dyer et al, 2009 p.3 reprint).

2. *Questioning*
Innovators persistently question the status quo. They ask bolder questions than executives who are simply improvement oriented. They are also considered to be better able to "hold opposing ideas in their head" (see the "new" leader in Chapter 1).

3. *Observing*
Acting like social scientists, innovators scrutinize observable stimuli more, particularly the behavior of consumers. Innovators focus on direct observation and observation of details.

4. *Experimenting*
Innovators engage in more experimentation at many levels, and as Dyer et al remark, "one of the most powerful experiments innovators can engage in is living and working overseas" (Dyer et al, 2009, p.6 reprint). Also, the more countries an executive has lived in, the more likely they are to use this experience to develop innovative products, processes or businesses. Hence my own findings on better strategic ability, higher confidence and social skills in internationally experienced executives are complemented by the positive effect on innovative capabilities advocated by these researchers.

5. *Networking*
Innovators seek out people with different perspectives to learn from other sectors or countries. They also use conferences or international gatherings that bring different people together to learn and to test some of their ideas. They build international and other networks on a proactive basis, as they are curious and try to absorb as many ideas and viewpoints as possible.

I worked with Gregersen at INSEAD in a leadership module on innovation and, as part of my own training, went through the Innovator's DNA Assessment. The results were interesting – the instrument clearly assesses dimensions that are not covered by other tools. It assesses the above five factors as well as "Challenging the Status Quo" and "Risk Taking". The instrument can be very effectively used in teams that are striving for innovation or in companies that require more innovation. Additionally, the Innovator's DNA also assesses *delivery* – evaluating whether individuals or teams are operationally fit enough to implement their innovative ideas, turning them into products.

6 Boards as Teams?

Governance versus Board Effectiveness

What should we aim for?

Ever since the Enron disaster, our traditional notion of corporate governance has been seriously questioned. How could a company previously hailed as a showcase for corporate governance lie, deceive and, in the end, go bust? Corporate governance has been under the spotlight since then and even more so since 2008: how could the boards of the largest financial institutions not have investigated the risk of its business practices more closely?

Are boards focusing on the wrong things in their effort to comply with the ever-increasing bureaucracy of corporate governance guidelines? On both sides of the Atlantic, regulatory pressures have intensified over the last couple of years and demand more and more time commitment from board directors. But as many have argued before, regulatory compliance is not enough and we need to look at the performance of boards.

What makes boards effective? What is a sound definition of a highly effective board and are there parallels to highly effective teams? (This question relates primarily to unitary boards.)

We are looking at this question in three ways:

1. The composition of boards: what is ideal?
2. The process of board work: what is the agenda and how is it tackled?
3. The dynamics of boards: the psychology, behavior and interaction of boards.

These are similar questions to those applied to top teams.

Board Composition

What is ideal?

At board level, we often see similar types of directors in terms of background, age and skills – rather homogenous groups. This has the advantage of predictability of performance and a low risk of conflict. In the past, many appointments were made through the old boys' network, restricting even further the range of board directors as far as class, gender and nationality are concerned.

With recent corporate governance developments, however, this has changed and the drive for greater transparency has influenced the selection processes of board directors to change the homogenous ("pale, male and stale") nature of many traditional boards to increasing board diversity. The diversity drive is at the forefront of board discussions in an attempt to bring more women on to boards and to internationalize boards; but what is the rationale?

Strategic selection

Similar to the argument around teams, we need a more strategic and systematic view of ideal board composition. A future-oriented analysis of business requirements, whether it is growth or turn-around oriented or a move into emerging markets, changes companies' selection of board members. Headhunters intuitively adopt this approach but, at times, they do not want to challenge long-standing clients or the status quo – they often provide a well-tested and rather conservative list of candidates. An in-depth analysis of competencies and experiences of the board will identify gaps and will facilitate more strategic appointments. Moreover, a more sophisticated analysis of key requirements will automatically expand the talent pool, as it forces everyone to look at a broader range of backgrounds and experiences. Therefore, a more detailed analysis of board requirements will automatically increase board diversity.

A Different View of Diversity

Diversity should ideally be looked at in a broader way, starting with demographics, such as age, gender, nationality, to different experiences, such as functional background, sector experience and international experience. This broader view of diversity or heterogeneity matches the diversity of business and markets. Taking an early interest in this topic, I started to look at board diversity in the late 1990s, with the question whether the best UK companies have unique boards. Looking at the Most Admired Companies in the FTSE 100 Index, I found that the composition of their boards was different from the rest (Marx, 1998). The boards of Britain's Most Admired Companies were more diverse in the broadest sense: they had broader functional experience, more international experience and more women. They were also larger and had a higher proportion of executive to non-executive directors. Interestingly, the last two characteristics were cited as in need of change by corporate governance experts, and boards nowadays are smaller in size and have a smaller number of executive directors.

But does the smaller size not restrict the scope for injecting diversity and does the larger number of non-executives make it more difficult to know the operational intricacies and the actual risks of the business? A comparison of the board profiles of the Most Admired Companies between 1996 and 2010 suggests that with regard to functional experience, board diversity has travelled backwards (Marx, 2011), as shown in Figure 6.1.

Looking at these figures, in real terms, boards have not advanced in all areas of diversity. The gains in the number of women and directors with international experience on boards are wiped out by the lack of diversity in functional background. In terms of functional background, board directors seem to have become more similar (i.e. more and more directors with an accountancy/finance background) rather than more diverse. A survey by KPMG in 2002 found that as many as 40 percent of non-executive directors questioned felt exposed on issues that went "beyond financial information" and commented that they lacked knowledge on environmental and political issues. Taking account of the massive increase in business complexity, I wonder what these statistics would look like at present? How many board directors have up-to-date knowledge and excellent judgement on environmental and political issues on a global scale?

Relating the steady increase of board directors with accountancy/finance backgrounds to Miles and Snow's Typology,

Figure 6.1 **Board comparison of Most Admired Companies (1996 versus 2010)**

one may ask whether the prevalence of throughput experience can instigate the growth that is so urgently needed in the UK? Or whether we have a sufficient number of ambidextrous leaders who can cut costs and start growth at the same time?

The changing profile of FTSE 100 CEOs since the economic crisis

If we compare the profiles of FTSE 100 CEOs before and after the start of the financial crisis, we find a two-track result. Whilst the talent pool is clearly widening in the appointment of non-British nationals, and a general increase in international experience, there is a narrowing in terms of career background.

The results are based on an analysis of profiles of FTSE 100 CEOs in 2010, and contrasting appointments pre-2008 with those made between 2008 and 2010. During this period, 35 percent of CEOs in the top 100 companies changed. The main findings are:

▷ 45 percent of CEOs appointed post-2008 were non-British, compared to 35.5 percent of CEOs prior to 2008. Almost one-third of the foreign CEOs are US nationals
▷ 54.5 percent of CEOs appointed post-2008 came from an accountancy/finance background, compared to 44.3 percent of CEOs appointed prior to 2008.

Boards have changed significantly in line with corporate governance directions to reduce the number of executive directors, but the subtler changes have clearly been harder to realize. In 1998, I argued that more diversity in terms of functional background on boards was necessary to deal with the complexity of international business. The results suggest that board diversity has not increased at the same pace as business complexity. The increasing importance of finance on boards shows the growing focus on the financial acumen of the board but raises the question whether this generates diversity in terms of perspectives, judgement and experiences as well as skills. Furthermore, does the increasing similarity in functional background indicate "group think" and a lack of challenge around the board table?

This opens a much larger and more important debate about what type of board is best equipped to deal with the current economic complexity. It also points to the pressing need to do more empirical research on the relationship between board composition and company performance.

Board Internationalization

Board internationalization is not only a trend in the UK but a trend in multinationals all over the world. This is also reflected in the statistics of recent international corporate governance studies.

Heidrick and Struggles' Corporate Governance report (2009) provides some very interesting European data on the topic.

In their 2009 survey, the three European countries with the largest percentage of non-national directors were:

▷ Netherlands (54 percent)
▷ Switzerland (45 percent)
▷ United Kingdom (41 percent).

The three European countries with the lowest percentage of non-national directors were:

▷ Italy (11 percent)
▷ Spain (10 percent)
▷ Germany (8 percent).

Only the Netherlands, Switzerland and the UK have truly pan-European boards, with non-nationals representing more than 40 percent of board members. Heidrick and Struggles commented in the same report that "the absence of non-national directors remains a challenge for many companies: one in four European boards includes no foreign directors at present and this proportion has remained stable over two years..." (p.13). Also, the majority of the international directors are Europeans, with the Asia Pacific region being underrepresented in contrast to the Asian expansion strategy of many European companies.

The board statistics in the US do not look much different – on the contrary. Egon Zehnder's 2008 study revealed the remarkable lack of international boards in the US. Of the 500 largest companies in the US, fewer than 10 percent had a foreign national board director. The top 100 companies in the 500 List are making some progress towards greater internationalization of the board but the next level of companies seems unaffected.

What do foreign board directors bring to the board?

One may argue they bring the following:

▷ knowledge of different markets and business practices
▷ customer knowledge in specific regions
▷ relationships with governments and other corporates (i.e. a "door opener")

6 ▶ BOARDS AS TEAMS?

▷ different strategic views
▷ understanding of values and behaviors in different settings.

Interviews with International Board Directors

How do international boards function?

The following interviews with board directors provide insights into their personal experiences with board internationalization.

Interview with Roxanne Decyk, US national and a board director on Petrofac PLC, a British FTSE 100 company (also independent director of Alliant Techsystems Inc. and of Snap-On in the US).

Most companies have definitely increased their appetite for international board directors. At Petrofac, we have a very interesting, culturally diverse board, with eight different countries represented. Companies are now looking for international perspectives or they are looking for particular regional or country experience. For example, board directors from China are extremely valuable for many Western companies if you can overcome the problem with the logistics of time and travel. As far as my own experience is concerned, I would say that my international board experience meets and even exceeds expectations; I can see the big advantage compared to mono-cultural boards for companies who operate across multiple countries or regions.

Directors who are asked to serve on boards outside of their home countries face challenges in addition to the expected governance accountabilities. How directors operate in a two-tier board, as for example on German boards, is very different from a one-tier board of the UK or the US. Another area in terms of cultural observations is what is an appropriate way to discuss difficult issues? Unless you have a very worldly group of board directors, there can be misunderstandings of intentions and meanings that are culturally driven and have absolutely nothing to do with any issues of competence. That means for an international board to be truly effective, it needs to develop a certain sophistication.

Induction of international board directors

In my own experience, I found that the Chairman and the Lead Director of Petrofac really stepped up and took extra efforts to accommodate me and to give me a very good induction. My advice is:

▷ first of all, spend extra time on onboarding to ensure that a foreign board director is completely prepared and oriented as to expected board behavior
▷ Secondly, if the board director comes from a very different background, it is important for the Chairman and the board to create opportunities for that individual to bring into the board conversation their different experience
▷ Thirdly, there is clearly also an onus on board directors who are seeking international appointments. You sometimes meet candidates who don't even know the basics regarding the governance requirements and structure of boards in different countries.

Michael Harper, Chairman of BBA Aviation PLC in the UK (also Chairman of Ricardo and Deputy Chairman of Qinetiq), comments on transatlantic boards:

As Chairman, I can say that the problem of managing board logistics increases significantly with international diversity, whether that is American or Asian board directors on European boards. It becomes more of a struggle to manage diaries as a one-day board meeting will easily involve three days' commitment when the travel of foreign board directors is considered.

US board directors on UK boards have to adapt to the differences in governance. The corporate governance environment in the US is different from the UK. UK Codes and Guidance and the role of brokers and investor relations advisers present different challenges to that of US regulation. US and UK practice and attitudes to pay levels, long- and short-term incentives, and performance conditions vary considerably. A Chairman needs to explain these differences to a new board director in terms of expectations.

Another difference is the attitude to pay and reward. Often board directors from the US are not familiar with the bonus conditions of executives in the UK and may think it unfair. This could cause misunderstandings and frictions on the Remuneration Committee. There is also a harsher

6 ▶ BOARDS AS TEAMS?

environment in the US – directors will always look at whether issues are regulated, and are inclined to move forward with many suggestions if the issue is not explicitly regulated. The US is much more litigious and most board directors will regularly consult their lawyer regarding their exposure on the board. This can obviously colour their approach to situations.

As a Chairman, I want to have directors with very different backgrounds and experience on board - reflecting the diversity of the business – but this also requires that the directors will be able to adapt and listen well.

Recommendations for the induction of non-nationals

The induction process should include meetings with the advisors to the company, including investor relations, brokers and lawyers. One of the best things we did was getting all our board directors together for a meeting and discussions with the brokers and investor relations. We also arranged a session with our law firm to provide more knowledge and understanding of the legal side, specific areas of legislation and to explain the liabilities in more detail.

There were also some behavioral differences between US and UK directors. US directors seem more willing to ask, challenge and push for certain ideas.

The remuneration of US directors on British boards can become an issue as UK companies pay their board directors less than US companies do and also they do not offer equity to board directors. I would also say that with transatlantic boards, the chairman needs to spend more time on communication and give regular interim updates between board meetings to keep everyone positively engaged. For BBA Aviation, as we have significant businesses in the US, it is logical for us to have a number of US board directors. This presents challenges but the benefits are real.

John McAdam, Non-Executive Director of Rolls-Royce, Senior Independent Director of Sainsbury, Chairman of United Utilities and of Rentokil, previously Independent Director of Sara Lee.

Strategic selection

The main recommendations I have is to be clear when you are appointing someone to the board what the person exactly brings to the board in addition to the required general business acumen, i.e. is it market knowledge, Government connections and so on. The selection of board directors is often still not strategic enough and should never be based on pure demographics.

Board talent and adaptability

The evaluation of foreign nationals can be tricky. If you do not have a general sense of internationalization, i.e. if you are not very international yourself, you may miss talent. To exaggerate the point, there could be a high risk of appointing a Brit-friendly non-national as opposed to a top French or German or Swiss business executive. You want enough understanding that will give you the comfort that the person will adapt as well. Overall, one needs to make special efforts in the interview and induction, and assessing the style and the adaptability of the board directors.

Jill Lee, Non-Executive Director of Sulzer AG (Switzerland), comments on her experience as the only Asian and the only woman director on the board: "The board at Sulzer is very interesting and it has a very good mix of nationalities and backgrounds and a very open discussion at the board table."

Practical recommendations regarding the induction of Asian board directors on European boards

First of all, it is helpful that the person has relevant international exposure to be able to benefit better from an induction program. I think if you do not have any relevant international experience, just relying on an onboarding program for preparation may be quite superficial.

Secondly, in order to adapt fast to the board, it certainly helps to be part of one or a couple of subcommittees. This facilitates a more intense exposure and makes sure that the foreign board director can learn and engage as fast as possible.

Thirdly, diversity clearly needs to be value-adding and be more than demographic considerations, i.e. boards need to be very clear why they have appointed you and what value you can contribute to the board composition and for the stage of the company.

6 ▶ BOARDS AS TEAMS?

> **Dr Utho Creusen, Non-Executive Director of Dixons PLC UK, Non-Executive Director of M.video Ltd (Russia) and Non-Executive Director of Mueller (Germany).**
>
> As a Dutch national, who has spent most of his executive career in Germany and now sits on UK, Russian and German boards, Utho Creusen has an interesting perspective on the internationalization of boardrooms.
>
> ## Language
>
> At Dixons, I started as the only non-UK board director and one of the challenges was the language. Although my English is very good, I can definitely not pick up the subtleties as fast as in my native language. This is different on the Russian board, as we have lots of nationalities, and the English that is used at board level is "international English" and every member of the board struggles to understand and to be understood.
>
> ## Onboarding experience
>
> I had an extremely well organized onboarding process. In one company, the Company Secretary gave me the first introduction. I also decided to take a short course at the Institute of Directors to understand the differences in corporate governance between the UK and, for example, German boards. Coming from Germany, the unitary board has a very different culture, with a higher team orientation and a stronger integration of board directors. It is probably operationally closer to the business.
> As this was my first foreign board position, I also took time to observe and understand the different styles and ways to express opinions. Getting to know every non-executive director and the key executives in one-to-one meetings was also very helpful to understand the company fast.
> An interesting initiative was suggested by one of my chairmen; he suggested sending him a list of questions I may have after reading the board papers so he understood the potential cultural differences.
>
> ## Emerging markets
>
> The situation is slightly different on boards in emerging markets. For example, in Moscow where M.video is based, there is a high trend for international board directors. Most companies that operate internationally have a high need to increase their international "know-how".

> As a foreigner, one also needs to make a decision whether the company is serious about foreign board directors, and whether their corporate governance practices are of a standard that one wants to be on the board. For example, I was very keen to understand that there is sufficient transparency and the quality of the executive team was very good, which was the case with M.video, before I accepted the position.
> One may be able to attract international calibre to the boards in the emerging markets, but then there's the question of how one deals with international talent. Do we develop the right organizational culture to integrate the talent? I personally find it incredibly interesting and rewarding to be on a combination of international and national boards.

Gender Diversity

Despite mounting pressure in Europe and the US to increase the number of women directors on boards, the progress has been painstakingly slow. The US organization Catalyst, which steers the drive for a more inclusive workplace, has researched and argued the business case for gender diversity for a long time. Its findings show a clear positive correlation between the number of women on boards and company performance in the US over time, although other research has failed to establish an unequivocal correlation.

Bilimoria's (2006) study in the US showed that the presence of women on boards is positively related with gender diversity in the top management team, suggesting companies that are serious about diversity should start at board level. Within the European context, Egon Zehnder's research (2010) shows wide variation regarding gender balance on boards. Analyzing 340 of the largest companies across 17 European countries, the Scandinavian countries have made the biggest progress, highlighted by 32 percent female board representation in Norway (which introduced a quota system some time ago) and 29 percent in Sweden and Finland. By contrast, Germany, Greece and Switzerland have only 8 percent to 10 percent of board seats allocated to women.

What does it take for women to get on to boards?

Instead of just looking at the statistics of women on boards, it is useful to look at the backgrounds and profiles of female board directors. If we understand what it takes for women to get to the top, we will also see what boards are looking for and how women might prepare and position themselves for future board roles. Analyzing the profiles of women board directors in Britain's largest companies, the findings revealed unique characteristics of board success (Marx, 2009). At the time of the study, there were 116 women on FTSE 100 boards, with only 18 in executive roles:

▷ 44 percent of these directors were foreign-born; 25 percent of this international group were US nationals
▷ More than two-thirds of the women had an advanced degree. Foreign-born women directors were more likely to have an advanced degree, generally an MBA, than British directors (83 percent versus 55 percent)
▷ A high proportion of the board directors had degrees from elite universities (Oxford or Cambridge in the UK, Ivy League universities in the US or the Grandes Écoles in France).

Career trends of the younger generation

Board directors of the largest companies are role models for any aspiring executive and particularly for the younger generation. The above research also showed that younger board directors (those below the age of 50) followed the outlined educational patterns even more strongly than their higher age counterparts (aged 55 and above):

62 percent of younger board directors were educated at elite universities, compared to 43 percent in the older group; and nearly 30 percent of the younger group had completed a degree abroad, hence they had more early international experience, compared to 11 percent in the higher age brackets.

Recommendations for women

Whilst the findings suggest educational pointers for the next generation, they should definitely not discourage women who do not possess these characteristics; rather they should help them to think about how they can structure their career and present their achievements. This can include:

▷ Executive committee involvement, either through full-time roles or strategic projects
▷ commercial and, ideally, P&L experience
▷ international work experience and business knowledge of specific countries or regions
▷ rare specialist knowledge that is relevant to specific industry sectors and functions
▷ increasing visibility through external networks, prestigious memberships and getting to know the chairmen or key influencers on boards (Marx 2009).

The diversity of nomination committees

If we all like to recruit in our own image, the diversity of the nomination committee seems a good starting point to address the lack of women on boards. In the above study (Marx 2009), boards with three or more women also had greater female representation on the nomination committee.

From my own discussions with chairmen, the board climate for women to progress has never been better throughout Europe. Chairmen are keen to facilitate this, not just because of political correctness but because they know that boardrooms need to attract talent in whatever form talent comes. An exclusive focus on women is too narrow and, as discussed at the beginning of this chapter, needs to be expanded to a broader definition of diversity. Ironically, a more strategic analysis of what a board needs in terms of skills and experience will automatically expand the talent pool, including that of female non-executive directors (Marx, 2011).

Getting the composition right is only the starting point for a successful board - a necessary but not sufficient condition for board effectiveness. How skills and diversity are applied in the boardroom and the dynamics of a successful board are the more interesting questions. And, ultimately, what is the impact of boards on business performance?

The Impact of Diversity

When does it make a difference?

The common assumption is that diversity has a positive impact. But diversity at the top will not automatically result in better company performance. This will depend on how that diversity is being used in the boardroom and whether board directors are open to being challenged by different perspectives and opinions. What board dynamics lead to superior performance? What are the performance indicators of a strong board?

As research on the dynamics of board diversity is scarce, let's first look at some interesting findings in relation to top management team diversity.

There is a number of studies looking at the effect of team heterogeneity on strategic outcomes, such as diversification, innovation and performance. Heterogeneity is measured by basic demographics. Demographics, whether age or functional or sector experience, are seen as a "proxy" for other types of diversity, for diversity in thinking. Most research in this area relies on studies of large numbers of teams. Yet, only if this large-scale research is complemented by in-depth case study approaches can we understand the real impact of diversity on top management teams and the critical importance that personality and power have on the outcome (Pitcher and Smith 2001). In other words, we need to get into the "black box" of the team and the board and analyze what is going on inside the boardroom. We may have findings that show a positive correlation between diversity and company performance but we do not know how this is achieved and we do not understand the processes and dynamics of getting there.

The impact of the leader on team diversity and business performance

Pitcher and Smith's study was based on an eight-year analysis of the board and management committee of a $20 billion global company in financial services. The top management team was comprised of the Chairman and CEO of the Group and of the divisional CEOs. Interviews with the CEOs and their teams focused on team functioning, strategy, structure, innovation, performance and the correlation of these factors with the personality of the Group CEO. Personality assessments of CEOs showed three types of leaders:

▷ the visionary, imaginative "artist"
▷ the stable, rational "craftsman"
▷ the hard-headed, detail-oriented "technocrat".

The TMT showed a good range of these personality types. As the Chairman was a visionary "artist" type, the strategic result was a focus on growth and expansion. Power seemed to be equally distributed as the divisional CEOs were autonomous. However, with the advent of a new chairman, who was a "technocrat", the power shifted and the growth goal changed into an efficiency drive. The new Chairman was seen as closed-minded and through his domineering leadership style, the "cognitive range" of the team declined over time and thus its cognitive diversity (as expressed in the variety of perspectives, ways of thinking and problem solutions) could not be realized. As a consequence, the strategic innovation slowed while the emphasis on systems and frameworks increased. The organization seemed to have become an "administrative beast".

Pitcher & Smith concluded that the lack of diversity that the TMT showed at the end "was inappropriate to the turbulent and competitive environment in which it operated, and the organization ultimately disappeared" (2001, p.16).

This case study shows the impact of the Chairman on company performance, and the importance of an in-depth understanding of personality and power at the top and their impact on the executive team. Manfred Kets de Vries, who is also a psychoanalyst, has written extensively on the personality of the business leader and its impact on the company (Kets de Vries, 2001): he identified a range of leadership types, including narcissistic leaders, controlling leaders and neurotic leaders, and discusses their impact in his book *The Leadership Mystique*.

As outlined in Chapter 3, in deciding whether a team intervention is indicated, I not only use the Top Team Health Check and interview the team members, but take a close look at the leader of the team. The personality of the leader is critical for the success of any intervention. It is often the best leaders who are interested in any systematic development of their teams as they are always improvement and change oriented. Open-mindedness, a willingness to question and a preparedness to change one's own behavior are some of the key indicators of leaders of teams that can be developed.

An interesting study by Zimmerman (2008) shows the effect of TMT heterogeneity on start-up valuations. Her findings suggest that functional and educational diversity in top teams is associated with greater capital raised through an IPO.

Diversity and Conflict

Another approach to understanding the "black box" of teams and boards and the effect of team diversity is illustrated in Amason's (1996) analysis of conflict resolution. According to his research on 63 top management teams, heterogeneity increases the conflict in teams, because of the range of different perspectives. Cognitive conflict (task-oriented disagreement arising from differences in perspective) is seen as positive if it contributes to finding better solutions. Unfortunately, cognitive conflict is often accompanied by affective conflict, i.e. disagreement resulting from personal disaffection, which manifests itself in such behaviour as personal reproaches or laying blame and hinders effective decision-making. The impact of positive (cognitive) and negative (affective) tension on the performance of a team has been illustrated in the case study of the financial services team in Chapter 3: the affective conflict that was caused by differences in thinking style in the London–New York team led to hostile behavior and scapegoating. This clearly impacted the team's performance – a large part of its energy was wasted and it ran the risk of neglecting its clients and the competition. The key to effective teamwork is therefore to manage both types of conflict.

Amason's research found that conflict improved decision quality but at the same time disrupts group affect. It can also make the implementation of decisions more difficult: a team may produce a brilliant solution but because of affective conflicts cannot implement it. Ongoing team conflicts weaken the energy and resilience of a team. Amason's conclusion is that decision-making and team work can be improved by encouraging the positive, task-oriented, cognitive conflict whilst discouraging the affective conflict – this is easier said than done.

A more in-depth follow-up study explored what factors influence cognitive and affective conflicts in teams (Amason and Sapienza, 1997). A business leader who is not able to manage and resolve ongoing conflicts in the team weakens his/her impact and weakens the team; he will also lose credibility. The effective leader recognizes the early signs of conflict in the team and manages conflicts actively. The successful leader contains the cognitive and affective tension of the team. Using the Culture Shock Triangle with teams, the cognitive and affective dimensions of the team become overt and the results often produce a light-bulb moment in the team as it understands the underlying psychological reasons for the conflict. Understanding the psychological pattern seems to "depersonalize" the conflict. This can then be the starting point to find more constructive ways to deal with differences and to establish some "behavioral rules" to discuss conflicting opinions.

In this way, a detailed psychological analysis of the team can help to understand and manage cognitive and affective conflicts. This "double-edged sword of cognitive and affective conflict" (Amason & Sapienza, 1997) suggests that heterogeneous teams need greater coordination and, consequently, better leaders than homogeneous teams. Moreover, one could also imagine that this "double-edged sword" may actually deter CEOs or chairmen from recruiting people who are "different".

Amason & Sapienza (1997) showed that team size positively correlated with cognitive and affective conflict. Openness was positively related to cognitive conflict, but also associated with greater affective conflict. The study is interesting in relation to boards. Since corporate governance in the UK recommended reducing the size of boards, between 1996 and 2010 the average board size has decreased (Marx, 2011). This may also have resulted in less cognitive diversity in an economy where complexity has steadily increased.

Further research by Mooney & Sonnenfeld (2001) emphasizes the factor of behavioral integration in teams. Heterogeneous teams with high behavioral integration (i.e. a higher level of teamyness) showed less affective conflict but also less cognitive conflict. Whilst less affective conflict is positive, does less cognitive conflict not imply less effective decision-making?

A team that has a real dialogue as opposed to a series of monologues typically has a leader who encourages openness and is prepared to reconcile conflicting views. Manfred Kets de Vries (2011) sees the ability to have a more open dialogue as a key factor in building high-performance teams. He equates this with having "courageous conversations" and describes them as follows:

> Courageous conversations are those less than pleasant exchanges... that are necessary to move people in the organization forward and away from inappropriate behavior. Courageous conversations occur when people are prepared and unafraid to say what they honestly think and feel to whom they need to say it, and to do so in a positive, constructive way so others can hear their message without judgement and respond to it in a similar manner. It is important to note that courageous conversations should be constructive and never hurtful (Kets de Vries, 2011, pp.196/97).

And of course, courageous conversations have never been more pressing than when businesses need to find new ways to adapt to changing circumstances.

How does a business leader deal with the conflicts that arise from diversity?

An interview with Evelyn Havasi, Managing Director of Citi, illustrates how her leadership style developed and how she learned to resolve conflicts in diverse teams.

The key challenges in managing international teams can be divided into four categories:

1. different personalities
2. different cultures

3. intergenerational and
4. unconscious bias.

These four operational or management challenges work together to impede the success of international teams. In one respect the only way to effectively address these challenges is to see every team member as an individual. There are two principles which act as my compass to guide my management style. First, treat others exactly as I would like to be treated. Second, inspiring an international team requires an in-depth understanding of the individuals in the team because one-size-fits-all management does not work. Building the understanding of personalities, cultures, intergenerational differences and the drivers of unconscious bias requires considerable effort. A manager makes deposits by advocating on behalf of the team, being transparent and building the trust of the team and creating a culture in which world-class talent can thrive on the values and vision embedded in the corporate fabric. The team deposits loyalty, work ethic and commitment and withdraws appreciation, understanding and financial compensation.

Firstly, let's take *personalities*. You may have some team members with dominant personalities. These individuals are very direct and goal oriented; they may be aggressive and love a conflict. If they interact with someone who is docile, or more consensus driven, this can produce conflict when they are executing together or trying to originate new business. This friction in the team must be addressed quickly and proactively by the team leader. Having observed this kind of conflict on numerous occasions, it is easy to recognize when to step in and intervene, drawing out each side and trying to encourage a finding of common ground.

Secondly, there is the *cultural divide*, and I submit that bankers in the US are less sensitive to different working styles than perhaps they should be. Insensitivity can easily be addressed by a team leader who helps team members from different cultures recognize that appreciating teams' complementary strengths far outweighs the negative implications of adjusting to different working styles. If professionals adapt with an open mind, incredible results can be obtained.

Thirdly, we have the *intergenerational conflict* that presents itself in all teams. Senior managers who remain unaware of what drives their younger team members are unable to develop their capabilities and maximize full potential. I observe two types of younger executives: one is the so-called entitlement generation, and the second is the less fortunate generation whose societal position shapes the manner in which they approach the workplace. The entitled generation has certain lifestyle expectations. The less fortunate generation is possessed of a certain fire in their belly with work ethic and motivation driving them forward. They each have very different views on what it takes to be successful and the energy they put into the work. This intergenerational conflict can similarly be solved by understanding the needs of the team members. What does it take to inspire them?

Fourth, we have *unconscious biases*. I have encountered unconscious bias in my career. Bias regarding gender and religious practice or my silent diversity have shaped the way in which I have been perceived by peers, senior managers, clients and team members. People do not expect women like me to be Type A, aggressive, strategic and at the same time be constrained by ritualistic constraints as an Orthodox Jew. I believe there are unconscious biases regarding religion, gender and age within US culture. This has sensitized me to even the slightest signs of discrimination, and as a consequence, I try to focus on respecting diversity, being responsive and I've also worked on diversity committees. In this way I have chosen to give back to those of my mentors who have opened doors for me, respected my diversity and respected my need for time off and being unconnected.

As I have faced unconscious bias in my career, I decided that I make the choices in how to react and whether I let others' bias undermine me. Despite all these challenges, I believe there are huge advantages of international teams. It is absolutely necessary for cross-border transactions to have a synthesis between European and Asian teams. Also, what I have observed is that despite all the cultural differences and sometimes the friction, teams can get over insensitivities when they have successes. One success fosters another and fosters a culture of loving to win. So, often it is best to concentrate on building the initial small successes in order for cultural differences to become less of an issue. As a leader, I try to lead by example and that means zero tolerance for absence of team work. Very often, you get individualists and highly competitive players who think they can only succeed by disadvantaging others around them. If that competitive behavior is rewarded, it creates a negative culture of backbiting. My own model for team working and steps to achieve this are as follows:

▷ Make sure that each team member can share their concerns and that I am personally approachable, supportive, as well as transparent with them
▷ I try to create a positive working environment where everybody is seen as being part of something bigger
▷ I try to be clear on the agenda. I think the indicators of one of the best international teams I've worked in are as follows: love to win, culture high trust and recognition.

Professor Randall Peterson at London Business School spent much of his career researching conflicts and conflict resolution. Instead of a group development model of neatly defined stages, he proposes that a better way of looking at team development is how conflicts are actively resolved. He sees conflicts as positive when managed well.

What drives groups forward is a conflict resolution oriented strategy. Most successful groups are actually those that develop by trying to figure out their ability to manage conflicts best. So group development is about conflict rather than a logical sequence (of stages). Conflict is the fundamental thing that drives changes in a group (Peterson, 2006).

According to Professor Peterson, what makes conflict resolution so difficult is that task conflicts easily turn into relationship conflicts, that is moving from "seeing the world differently" to "hate you" (personal communication). This negative turn is less likely to happen in teams that have established trust, raising the fundamental issue on how to instill trust. And in his view, this is through effective team governance with clear decision-making rules.

His view is that "you have to have diversity in the best teams but it has to be well managed. A diverse team badly managed is worse than a homogenous team" (personal communication, 2013). And this brings us back to the quality of leadership.

Having high-calibre non-executive directors is only the starting point of an effective board – the psychology of the chairman and the psychology of the other board members and their interplay will determine how effectively the board operates. Corporate governance guidelines are, of course, necessary but they may have become an end in itself rather than a means to an end – the end being a high-performing board that makes use of its diversity, has an understanding of the difference of power and authority, and is aware of its own defence mechanisms in dealing with negative information and risk.

The Psychology of Boards

What are the implications for practice? Some writers equate the topic of cognitive conflict with Pandora's Box: once it is open, it becomes uncontrollable – the original conflict may easily widen and turn into serious negative dynamics, as we have seen in some previous examples.

What are the conditions that allow teams and boards to engage in constructive problem-solving whilst reducing the risk of affective tensions? According to Kets de Vries (2011), the most effective leader of a team (or a board for that matter) is able to "contain the emotions" of the group. Psychoanalytic and group dynamic theories provide excellent frameworks and ways to understand what is playing out in interactions at a conscious and unconscious level and some of these are lucidly explained in Kets de Vries' book on high-performance teams (*The Hedgehog Effect*, 2011).

Following the collapse of Lehman's and the government bailout of some of Britain's largest banks, including Royal Bank of Scotland and Lloyds, Sir David Walker, the Chairman of Barclays, was asked by the UK government to conduct a review of corporate governance of UK banking industry and outline recommendations to improve governance.

His recommendations in November 2009 were widely discussed and had an impact on all sectors. Surprisingly, The Walker Review included an annex on "Psychological and Behavioral Elements in Board Performance" – a summary of psychological issues related to board performance by the Tavistock Institute of Human Relations and Crelos Ltd.

Their recommendations start with the qualities of the leader and distinguishes the key characteristics of an effective chairman as follows:

1. integrating the board's collective thinking
2. empathy and promoting openness in board members
3. facilitating interactions
4. developing others
5. communicating complex messages succinctly
6. collaborating across boundaries
7. continuous improvement.

They argue that "a chairman's behavior must operate at a number of levels – task, group, and systemic" (The Walker Review, 2009, p.140). These guidelines mirror the characteristics of an effective team leader rather than the characteristics of a remote chairman – the parallels between leading the board and leading an executive team become even more transparent when they write "effective leadership of group involves holding a balance between satisfying the group's emotional needs and holding the group to 'work'" (p.143). This concept is similar to Kets de Vries' assumption that effective leaders provide emotional containment of the group. Moreover, Kets de Vries asserts "the most effective people interested in creating high performance teams are unafraid of incertitude and unresolved issues and are able to remain open-minded" (2011, p.151). And the best chairmen I know do exactly both of these things.

Moreover, similar to my recommendations with executive teams, the suggestions include:

▷ The chairman, non-executive and executive directors should be assessed at appointment and annually. This should include a full psychological assessment of behavior, experience, knowledge, motivation and intellect. This ongoing review would also address the question whether the board is effective for different business scenarios. How practicable this is in today's business is questionable. My personal view is to encourage chairmen to engage in some form of development which is confidential and highly tailored; similar to many CEO developments. A psychological assessment can certainly help the chairman to understand his/her own behavior and impact, including the way he or she deals with conflicts, risks and power. This could also include some training in group psychology, group think and group dynamics.

The development of chairmen should also be considered given some informal comments on their effectiveness. When I asked a number of chairmen of public companies what percentage of chairmen they would consider really effective, they suggested a disappointing 25 percent.

▷ All members should be trained in how to take up roles, managing role boundaries, the difference between power and authority and group dynamics.

▷ Boards with more than twelve people become ineffective in their view, as "the span of attention, the ability to deal with complexity and the ability to maintain effective interpersonal relationships and motivation are compromised." They recommend the optimum size of boards between eight and twelve (similar to teams) and subcommittees between five and nine.

This last point mirrors the pattern of teams. It focuses on a closer collaboration, beyond a "working group" that comes together primarily to exchange information. If this is the ideal type scenario, then a new definition of corporate effectiveness as "behavioral governance" could be considered and a behavioral framework of effectiveness could be developed. Similar to the comments on the Upper Echelon Theory, we have to open up the "black box" and understand the behavior of the best boards to outline specific recommendations to improve the behavioral governance. And a behavioral view of the board starts with a better understanding of the ideal profile of the chairman.

The Tavistock and Crelos' submission to The Walker Report speaks of transformational leadership in chairmen - leaders who know how to listen, provide synthesis, have subtle influencing skills and can sense what lies behind individual statements – chairmen that can deal with different personalities, views and values in the boardroom.

Chris Pierce, the CEO of Global Governance Services, has the following observations on chairmen:

> The role of the chairman is becoming more and more prominent, particularly through the recent surge in board evaluations. My observation is that the competence frameworks for chief executives and chairmen are totally different and there is a question whether chief executives will in fact make good chairmen. The most convincing attributes for an effective chairman are high emotional intelligence and the ability to interface with others - not management expertise or results orientation. Before the financial crisis, chairmen were almost invisible but this has changed and they have become much more prominent externally.
>
> What I see in my consulting work with international boards is that the interpretation of risk and the approach towards risk is very different in different countries. To ascertain risk nowadays, you have to have a wide knowledge of global context and of politics and general practices. Training and development is useful but you also need to have certain personality attributes to be flexible and to deal with this. Boards should probably spend much more time on issues

of risk appetite and risk tolerance, and review management and control processes in this context.

One of the criticisms of financial services boards pre-Lehman is whether they engaged in sufficient debate and whether the issue of risk was sufficiently prominent. Paraphrasing the title of a recent *Financial Times* article by John Kay (8 December 2012), boards need to learn to love the candid bearer of bad news. We know from psychological research that individuals react differently to negative information or threat: whereas some of us go towards it and want more and more information (called sensitizers in psychological literature), others repress negative information and pretend nothing has happened (the repressors).

Risky decision-making in groups

One phenomenon to be aware of with executive teams or boards making decisions is the "Risky Shift Phenomenon". Group discussions lead to more hazardous decisions compared to individuals making decisions on their own. Riskiness is positively viewed in the West and, therefore, individuals want to take as much risk as their peers, and in a group they will move to a more extreme position to make sure they do not lag behind the others. Given the disastrous risky decisions of several executive teams at the top banks, this may be a useful group fact to be aware of for many teams in future.

The Future of Boards – Behavioral Governance

To understand the impact of boards, we need access to boardrooms. Andrew Pettigrew of Oxford's Saïd Business School has consistently argued that we need to understand the board process and not simply focus on content and outcome. His research provides a unique insight into strategy impact of board members. Interviewing 108 board directors of British public companies, he found that board directors are involved in strategy development in three different ways:

1. Taking strategic decisions
2. Shaping strategic decisions – where non-executive directors influence the decision-making process early on

3. Shaping the content, context and conduct of strategy – where the influence is continuous and not confined to decision episodes (McNulty and Pettigrew, 1999, p.55).

These three ways indicate different levels of interaction between the non-executive and the executive directors. Does Level 3 (which is closest to a team-oriented approach) result in more effective strategic decision-making, better adaptation and greater results for the company? What do the best board interactions look like? Future research clearly needs to analyze the interior of the boardroom and understand the behavioral dynamics that will produce high performance in a global world.

Bibliography

Amason, A.C. (1996) "Distinguishing the Effects of Functional and Dysfunctional Conflict on Strategic Decision Making: Resolving a Paradox for Top Management Teams," *Academy of Management Journal*, 39: 123–145.

Amason, A.C. and Sapienza, H.J. (1997) "The Effects of Top Management Team Size and Interaction Norms on Cognitive and Affective Conflict," *Journal of Management*, 23: 495–517.

Belbin, M.R. (1993) *Team Roles at Work*, London: Butterworth-Heinemann.

Bem, S. (1974) "The Measurement of Psychological Androgyny," *Journal of Consulting and Clinical Psychology*, 42: 155–162.

Berry, J.W., Poortinga, Y.H., Segall, M.H., Dasen, P.R. (2002) *Cross-Cultural Psychology: Research and Applications*, Cambridge: Cambridge University Press.

Bilimoria, D. (2006) "The Relationship Between Women Corporate Directors and Women Corporate Officers," *Journal of Management Issues*, 18(1): 47–61.

Brimm, L. (2010) *Global Cosmopolitans*, London: Palgrave Macmillan.

Citrin, J.M. and Ogden, D. (2010) "Succeeding at Succession," *Harvard Business Review*, 29–31, November 2010.

Collins, J. (2001) *Good to Great*, London: Random House.

Dyer, J.H., Gregersen, H.B. and Christensen, C.M. (2009) "The Innovator's DNA," *Harvard Business Review*, December 2009.

Egon Zehnder International (2008) *Global Board Index*, A Board Report.

Egon Zehnder International (2010) *European Board Diversity Analysis 2010*, A Board Report.

Ekman, P. (1973) *Darwin and Facial Expression; a Century of Research in Review*, Waltham, Mass.: Academic Press.

Fredrickson, B.L. and Losada, M. (2005) "Positive Affect and the Complex Dynamics of Human Flourishing," *American Psychologist*, 60 (7): 678–686.

Freeland, C. (2011) "The Rise and Fall of the New Global Elite," *The Atlantic*, January/February 2011.

Goleman, D. (1996) *Emotional Intelligence*, London: Bloomsbury.

Gratton, L. and Erickson, T.J. (2007) "Eight Ways to Build a Collaborative Team," *Harvard Business Review*, 100–109, November 2007.

Hambrick, D. (2001) "Upper Echelons: Donald Hambrick on Executives and Strategy," *Academy of Management Executive*, 15 (3).

Hambrick, D.C. and Mason, P.A. (1984) "Upper Echelons: the Organization as a Reflection of its Top Managers," *Academy of Management Review*, 9: 193–206.

Hansen, M.T. and Ibarra, H. (2010) "The Best Performing CEOs in the World," *Harvard Business Review*, 1–9, January 2010.

Harré, R. and Parrott, W.G. (1996) *Emotions: the Social, Cultural and Physical Dimensions*, London: Sage.

Hefferon, K. and Boniwell, J. (2011) *Positive Psychology. Theory, Research and Applications*, Maidenhead: McGraw-Hill.

Heidrick & Struggles (2009) *Boards in Turbulent Times*, A Corporate Governance Report.

Herrmann, P. and Datta, D.K. (2005) "Relationships Between Top Management Team Characteristics and International Diversification: an Empirical Investigation," *British Journal of Management*, 16: 69–78.

Hofstede, G. (1994) *Cultures and Organizations*, London: HarperCollins.

Kahnemann, D. (2011) *Thinking, Fast and Slow*, London: Allen Lane.

Katzenbach, J.R. and Smith, D.K. (1993) *The Wisdom of Teams*, Boston: Harvard Business School Press.

Katzenbach, J.R. and Smith, D.K. (1993a) "The Discipline of Teams," *Harvard Business Review*, 162–171.

Kay, J. (2011) *Obliquity. Why Our Goals are Best Achieved Indirectly*, London: Profile Books.

Kets de Vries, M.F.R. (2001) *The Leadership Mystique*, London: Financial Times/Prentice Hall.

Kets de Vries, M.F.R. (2012) "Star Performers: Paradoxes Wrapped Up in Enigmas," *Organizational Dynamics*, 41: 173–182.

Kets de Vries, M.F.R. (2006) "*Decoding the Team Conundrum: The Eight Roles Executives Play*," INSEAD working paper.

Kets de Vries, M.F.R. (2011) *The Hedgehog Effect. Executive Coaching and the Secrets of Building High-Performance Teams*, San Francisco: Jossey-Bass.

Khurana, R. (2001) "Finding the Right CEO: Why Boards Often Make Poor Choices," *MIT Sloan Management Review*, 91–95.

Lawrence, B.S. (1997) Perspective – the Black Box of Organizational Demography, *Organization Science*, 8: 1, January–February, 1–22.

Lazarus, R.S. (1966) *Psychological Stress and the Coping Process*, New York: McGraw-Hill.

Lewis, R. (1996) *When Cultures Collide*, London: Nicholas Brealey.

Lonner, W. (1990) "An Overview of Cross Cultural Testing and Assessment," in R.W. Brislin (ed.) *Applied Cross Cultural Psychology*, Newbury Park, CA: Sage.

Marx, E. (1996) *The International Manager*, A report by NB Selection.

Marx, E. (1996) *The Move to the Top – Career Profiles of CEOs in the Top 100 Companies*, A report by Norman Broadbent.

Marx, E. (1998) *A View at the Top – Boardroom Trends in Britain's Top 100 Companies*, A report by Norman Broadbent.

Marx, E. (2001) *Breaking Through Culture Shock: What You Need to Succeed in International Business*, London: Nicholas Brealey.

Marx, E. (2001) "Best Practice for Boards," *Financial Times*, 10 October 2001.

Marx, E. (2004) "Developing Global Leaders," *International Management Quarterly*, 6–7.

Marx, E. and Tappin, S. (2006) "Leadership – Managing Paradox," *Management Today*, September 2006.

Marx, E. (2008) *Route to the Top. A Transatlantic Comparison of Business Leaders*, A report by Heidrick & Struggles.

Marx, E. (2009) *Route to the Top. What Does it Take for Women to Get on to FTSE 100 Boards?*, A report by Heidrick & Struggles.

Marx, E. (2011) "Beyond Gender Diversity," *Financial Times*, 26 May 2011.

Miles, R.E. and Snow, C.C. (1978) *Organization Strategy, Structure and Process*, New York: McGraw-Hill.

Misumi, R. (1985) *The Behavioral Science of Leadership*, Ann Arbor, MI: University of Michigan Press.

McNulty, T. and Pettigrew, A. (1999) "Strategists on the Board," *Organization Studies*, 47–74.

Mooney, A.C. and Sonnenfeld, J. (2001) "Exploring Antecedents to Conflict During Strategic Decision Making: The importance of Behavioral Integration," *Academy of Management Best Paper Proceedings*.

Oberg, K. (1960) "Culture Shock: Adjustment to New Cultural Environments," *Practical Anthropology*, 7: 177–182.

Olsen, B., Parayitam, S., Twigg, N. (2006) "Mediating Role of Strategic Choice Between Top Management Team Diversity and Firm Performance: Upper Echelons Theory Revisited," *Journal of Business and Management*, 12(2): 111–126.

Peterson, R. (2007) "Bullies Need not Apply," *Business Strategy Review*, London Business School, Summer 2007.

Pink, D. (2005) *A Whole New Mind*, New York: Riverhead Books.

Pitcher, P. and Smith, A. (2001) "Top Management Team Heterogeneity: Personality, Power, and Proxies," *Organization Science*, 12: 1–18.

Rosen, R. and Adair, F. (2007) "CEOs Misperceive Top Teams' Performance," *Harvard Business Review*, September 2007.

Rosen, R. and Adair, F. (2008) "Top Management Teams and their Discontent," *Chief Executive*, July/August 2008.

Schein, E.H. (1985) *Organizational Culture and Leadership: A Dynamic View*, San Francisco: Jossey-Bass.

Solberg, A.G. (2008) "Androgynous Leaders Mean Increased Innovation," *Science News*, 7 November 2008.

Sussman, N.M. and Rosenfeld, H.M. (1982) "Influence of Culture, Language and Sex on Conversational Distance," *Journal of Personality and Social Psychology*, 42: 66–74.

Thomas, A.S. and Ramaswamy, K. (1996) "Matching Managers to Strategy: Further Tests of the Miles and Snow Typology," *British Journal of Management*, 7: 247–261.

Trompenaars, F. (1993) *Riding the Waves of Culture*, London: Nicholas Brealey.

Tugdale, M.M. and Fredrickson, B.L. (2004) "Resilient Individuals Use Positive Emotions to Bounce Back from Negative Emotional Experiences," *Journal of Personality and Social Psychology*, 86: 320–333.

Walker, D. (2009) *The Walker Review of Corporate Governance of UK Banking Industry*, November 2009.

Zimmerman, M.A. (2008) "The Influence of Top Management Team Heterogeneity on the Capital Raised Through an Initial Public Offering," *Entrepreneurship Theory and Practice*, 32 (3): 391–414.

Index

Bold entries refer to figures and tables.

ABB, 64–5
acculturation, 52–3, 105, 114–15
Acumen Fund, 40
Adair, Fred, 27
adaptability, and Chinese culture, 122, 124
Adjaye, David, 20
advertising business, 89–90
affective conflict, 173, 174–5
Amason, A. C., 173–4
ambidextrous firms, 43
ambiguity, and tolerance of, 57–8, 59, 127
ambition, and impact on team effectiveness, 78
AMEC, and diversity agenda, 64
see also Brikho, Samir
American Management Association, 5
Amnabi, Mukesh, 135
analyzer organizations, 38, 42, 43
androgyny, psychological, 17–20
Apollo syndrome, 6
Apte, Shirish, 2, 54
  and Asian markets, 65–6, 116–17
  and conflict resolution, 67
  and creating effective global teams, 67
  and differences between Asian and European teams, 67
  and global teams in financial services, 47–50
  and team leaders, 68
Ashridge Strategic Management Centre, 39
Asia
  and business culture, 59, 116–17
  and characteristics of markets in, 65–6
  and differences between Asian and European teams, 66
  and leadership characteristics, 125
associating, and innovation, 154–5
auction business
  and challenges in managing international teams, 87
  and managing star performers, 86–7
  and succession management, 88
awareness training, 119–20

Barclays
  and culture change, 23–6
  see also Jenkins, Antony
BBA Aviation plc, 164–5
behavioral governance, 181, 182–3
Belbin, M. R., 6
Bem, Sandra, 18

Berkett, Neil, 102, 121,
    126–30
  and aligning leaders to
    purpose, 127–8
  and attracting great leaders,
    126–7
  and building resilience, 129
  and career of, 126
  and creating great leaders,
    128–9
  and cultural characteristics of
    Virgin Media, 129
  and development as CEO,
    128–9
  and diversity, 130
  and leadership style, 129
  and well-functioning teams,
    130
Berry, J. W., 96, 97
biases, unconscious, 115,
    147–8, 177
  and halo effect, 148
Bilimoria, D., 168
board of directors, 4
  and assessment of members,
    180
  and behavioral governance,
    181, 182–3
  and best practices in CEO
    selection, 133–4
  and characteristics of effective
    chairman, 179–80, 181
  and composition of:
    drive for diversity, 158;
    homogeneity of, 158;
    strategic selection, 158
  and diversity, 158–60;
    conflict management,
    173–5; decline in, 159;
    positive effect of 7–8
  and effectiveness of, 157
  and gender diversity, 168;
    characteristics of women
    board members, 168–9;
    nomination committees,
    170; recommendations for
    women, 169–70
  and internationalization
    of, 161–2; adaptability,
    166; benefits of, 162–3;
    directors' experiences with,
    163–8; emerging markets,
    167–8; induction of
    non-nationals, 164,
    165, 166, 167; language
    problems, 167; strategic
    selection, 165–6
  and psychology of, 178–82
  and risk assessment, 181–2
  and role of chairman, 181
  and selection of CEOs,
    132–3, 136
  and size of, 159, 174, 180–1;
    reduction in executive
    directors, 159, 161
  and strategy development,
    182–3
  and Walker Review
    recommendations, 180–1
Boniwell, J., 152, 153
Branson, Richard, 126
Brikho, Samir, 2
  and developing international
    teams, 63–5
  and development as leader,
    30, 31
  and diversity, 64
  and profile of, 9–10
Brimm, Linda, 59
business cultures, differences
    in, *see* cultural
    differences

▶ INDEX

Campbell, Andrew, 39–40
career development, and
    Executive Team Reviews,
    144
Catalyst, 168
CEOs (Chief Executive Officers)
    and average tenure of, 131
    and best practices in selection
        of, 133–4
    and criteria in search for, **8**–9
    and cultural differences in
        functional backgrounds
        of, 41
    and factors affecting success
        of, 44, 134, 135–6
    and foreign-born, 60, 161
    and "hero" model of
        leadership, 5
    and influence of economic
        conditions at start of
        career, 136
    and international comparison
        of performance of, 134–5
    and international experience,
        10–11, 59–60
    and international literacy,
        10–11
    and narrowing of career
        background, 160–1
    and perceptions of team
        effectiveness, 1, 27
    and selection failures, 35
    see also search and selection
        processes; succession
        management
Chambers, John, 135
change, and management of,
    93, 96
Chang Weining, 121–3
Chief Executive Officers, *see*
    CEOs

Chief Financial Officer (CFO),
    6
Chief Operating Officer
    (COO), 6
China, 65
    and adaptability, 122, 124
    and business culture, 59, 116,
        117
    and characteristics of leaders
        and teams, 124–6
    and flexibility of coping, 123
    and growth in confidence, 125
    and management of
        emotions, 123
    and pragmatism, 124
    and resilience of leaders, 122–3
    and response to volatility,
        122–3
    and Singapore's approach to,
        117
    and situational attunedness,
        123
    and view of self, 122
Christie's Asia, *see* Curiel,
    François
Citi Asia, *see* Apte, Shirish
coaching, and team
    development, 46
cognitive conflict, 173, 174–5,
    178–9
collaboration
    and rudimentary level of, 26
    and team effectiveness, 24,
        25
collectivist societies, 19
    and business culture, 56, 57
Collins, Jim, 16, 61
communication styles
    and cultural differences, 59,
        104, 149
    and team development, 114

communitarianism, and business culture, 57
company performance
  and characteristics of top management team, 132
  and diversity, 7, 171
  and gender diversity, 7-8, 168
  and impact of team development intervention, 82, 112
  and leadership styles, 121
  and match between executive characteristics and strategy, 42
  and mergers, 94
  and psychology-context-strategy model of team development, 51
competency assessments, 145-6
competitiveness, and team effectiveness, 78, 177
complementarity, and team composition, 6
complexity, and international business, 6, 14
conflict management, 25, 102
  and affective conflict, 173, 174-5
  and benefits of conflict, 178
  and cognitive conflict, 173, 174-5, 178-9
  and creating global teams, 67
  and diversity, 173-5, 176-7, 178; intergenerational conflict, 176-7; personalities, 176
Confucius, 122
cooperation, and leadership style, 22-3
corporate governance
  and questioning of notions of, 157
  and Walker Review, 179-81
courageous conversations, 175
Crelos Ltd, 179, 181
Creusen, Utho, 167-8
cultural change, 106-7
  and acculturation, 52-3, 105, 114-15
  and Antony Jenkins at Barclays, 23-6
  and emotions, 97
  and governance, 98-9
  and innovation, 113-14
  and mergers, 96
  and psychological adaptation, 96-7
  and socio-cultural adaptation, 96-7
  and starting from the top, 96, 107
  see also turnaround case study
cultural differences, 55-9
  and acculturation, 52-3, 105, 114-15
  and Asia, 116-17
  and communication styles, 59, 104, 149
  and dimensions of, 116
  and emotional expression, 104-5
  and frameworks vs flexibility, 57-9
  and Germany, UK and China comparison, 116, 117
  and global team development, 76
  and mergers, 92
  and neutral vs emotional communication style, 59
  and psychological assessments, 150-1
  and task vs people orientation, 56-7

INDEX

and unconscious basic
   assumptions, 115
and work/life overlap, 103–4
culture
   and definition of, 73
   and means of expressing, 73
culture shock
   and dealing with, 75
   in global teams, 52–3
   and indicators of, 53
   and managing, 53
   and meaning of, 53
   and mergers, 93, 94, **95**
Culture Shock Triangle, 11–**12**
   and agility, 20–1
   and applications of, 12–13
   and differences in business cultures, 56–9
   as framework for global leadership development, 75
   and managing emotional side of, 53–4
   and managing paradoxes, 16–17
   and managing thinking side of, 54–5
   and psychological dimensions of, **74**
   and resilience, 14–15, 53–4
Curiel, François, 2, 85–8
   and career of, 85
   and challenges in managing international teams, 87
   and lessons learned in managing international teams, 87–8
   and managing star performers, 86–7

Datta, D. K., 132
decision-making
   and conflict, 173–4, 175
   and emotions, 3, 15
   and risky decision-making in groups, 182
Decyk, Roxanne, 163–4
defender organizations, 38
   and executive characteristics, 42
   and strengths of, 39
Diageo, 133
dialogue, and team effectiveness, 33, 175
diversity
   and analyzer organizations, 43
   and board membership, 158–60
   and broad view of, 158–9
   and business culture, 114–16
   and challenge of diverse teams, 69
   and company performance, 7, 168, 171
   and conflict management, 173–5, 176–7, 178; intergenerational conflict, 176–7; personalities, 176
   and culture shock, 53
   and global team development, 51, 64
   and managing emotional side of, 53–4
   and managing thinking side of, 54–5
   and measurement of, 171
   and narrowing of CEOs career backgrounds, 160–1
   and team composition, 6–7
   and team effectiveness, 7
   and top management teams, 171
Dixons plc, 167
Durkheim, Emile, 90

Dyer, J. H., 154–5
dynamics, and team
  development, 32
  and financial services, 47–50
  and global team
    development, 45–50
  and Rockefeller Foundation,
    45–7

Ekman, Paul, 104
emerging markets
  and building an international
    business in, 63–5
  and internationalization of
    boards, 167–8
emotions
  and business cultures, 59
  and Chinese management of,
    123
  and cultural change, 97
  and cultural differences in
    display of, 104–5
  and Culture Shock Triangle,
    12
  and decision-making, 3, 15
  and emotional awareness, 75
  and emotional intelligence, 60
  and global economic crisis,
    14–15
  and international business, 13
  and lack of focus on, 97
  and management of, 153–4
  and negative impact of, 75
  and problem-solving, 119
  and resilience, 15, 53–4, 119,
    154
  and self-evaluation checklist,
    22
  and self-management of, 118
  in teams, 75
  and universality of, 104–5
Enron, 157

Erickson, T. J., 7, 68, 69
Europe
  and communication styles, 59
  and differences between teams
    in Europe and Asia, 66
  and gender diversity on
    boards, 168
  and non-national directors,
    161–2
Executive Team Reviews,
  136–7
  and assessment methods,
    144–5
  and career development, 144
  and characteristics of
    innovators, 154–6
  and competency assessments,
    145–6
  and financial services firm
    case study, 137–8; benefits
    of review, 141; elements
    of review, 138–9; key
    findings of, 140–1
  and international expansion,
    143–4
  and international merger,
    142–3
  and psychological
    assessments, 146–7; cross-
    cultural assessments,
    150–1; cross-cultural
    differences in acceptability
    of, 147; factors affecting
    value of, 149–50
  and strengths-based
    assessment, 152–3
  and succession management,
    142
  and 360° feedback, 151–2
experimentation, and
  innovation, 155
extraverts, 103

facial expressions, and cultural differences, 104-5
financial services, team development in, 47-50, 70
and action-oriented approach, 73-4
and common goals of team members, 72, 73
and cultural differences, 71, 80
and Culture Shock Triangle, 74-5
and key steps in, 76
and linking approach with individual goals, 81
and problems with existing approach, 70-1
and psychological component, 78-9
and psychology-context-strategy model of, 73, **74**
and requirements for success, 71-3
and results of, 82
and strategy, 78
and team profile, 78-9
and two-fold approach to, 73
and understanding cross-cultural differences, 76
and using quantitative indicators, 72, 81
and workshops, 81-2
Finland, and gender diversity, 168
Fitzgerald, F. Scott, 16
France, and business culture, 57
Fredrickson, B. L., 153
Freeland, Chrystia, 21

Geitner, Thomas, 112-14, 149
and career of, 112
and cultural change, 113-14
and governance, 112
and innovation, 113-14
and leadership challenges, 114
and recruiting for future needs, 113
and trust, 113
gender diversity
and board membership, 168; characteristics of women board members, 168-9; nomination committees, 170; recommendations for women, 169-70
and company performance, 7-8, 168
General Electric, 133
Germany
and business culture, 57, 116, **117**
and gender diversity, 168
and non-national directors, 162
Gilbert, Samantha, and Rockefeller Foundation, 45-7
GlaxoSmithKline, 133
global economic crisis, and emotional impact of, 14-15
Global Executive Leadership Inventory (GELI), 151-2
Global Governance Services, 181
Goleman, Daniel, 60
governance, and team development, 32-4, 106, 112
and checklist questions, 33
and definition of a team, 33
and innovation, 113-14
and need for clarity, 100
and reality of governance in executive teams, 101-4

governance, and team
    development – *continued*
    and recommendations for, 33
    see also behavioral
    governance; corporate
    governance; turnaround
    case study; Virgin Media
Gratton, L., 7, 68, 69
Greece, and gender diversity, 168
Gregersen, Hal, 154–6

halo effect, 148
Hambrick, D. C., 38, 42, 43, 132
Hansen, M. T., 135
Harper, Michael, 164–5
Harré, R., 59
Havasi, Evelyn, 103, 175–7
Hefferon, K., 152, 153
Heidrick and Struggles, 1, 27, 161–2
Herrmann, P., 132
Hewlett Packard, 5, 35
high-performance teams
    and characteristics of, 100, 153
    and definition of, 34
    and group flow, 153
Hofstede, G., 55–6, 57, 73
HSBC, 54–5
hybrid organizations, 131

Ibarra, H., 135
identity
    and global leaders, 20–1
    and transnational community, 60
Immelt, Jeff, 133
individualistic societies, and business culture, 56
innovation
    and characteristics of innovators, 154–6
    and cultural change, 113–14
    and governance, 113–14
INSEAD's Global Leadership Centre (IGLC), 6, 19, 151–2, 154
intergenerational conflict, 176–7
international expansion, and Executive Team Reviews, 143–4
international experience
    and CEOs, 10–11, 59–60
    and positive effects of, 62, 154, 155
international literacy
    and emotion management, 13
    and global leadership, 10–11
    and international experience, 10–11, 59–60
    and new leadership, 10–11
interpersonal skills
    and challenging the team, 102
    and effective leadership, 60–2
introverts, 103
Italy
    and business culture, 59
    and non-national directors, 162

Jaguar Land Rover, 93
Japan
    and business culture, 59
    and emotional expression, 104–5
Jenkins, Antony, 2, 23
    and culture change, 23–6
Jobs, Steve, 18, 135, 155
John Lewis Partnership, 16
Jung, Carl, 17

Kahnemann, Daniel, 15
Katzenbach, J. R., 32–4, 100, 101, 105, 106

Katzenbach Partners, 32
Kay, John, 58, 182
Kets de Vries, Manfred
  and courageous
    conversations, 175
  and effective leadership, 179,
    180
  and Global Executive
    Leadership Inventory
    (GELI), 151–2
  and leadership types, 172
  and "Star Performers", 17
  and team types, 6–7
Khurana, Rakesh, 35–6

languages
  and developing proficiency
    in, 65
  in international teams, 114
  and non-national directors,
    167
Lazarus, R. S., 119
leadership
  and agility, 20–1
  and behavior and social skills,
    60–2
  and challenges of, 8
  and changed criteria for, 2
  and characteristics of effective
    leaders, 179–80
  and competencies and skills, 9
  and conflict management,
    174; intergenerational
    conflict, 176–7;
    personalities, 176
  and criteria in CEO search,
    8–9
  and Culture Shock Triangle,
    11–12
  and development of, 11
  and emotion management,
    153, 154
  and expanded notion of, 5–6
  and global leadership, 10–11
  and global nomads, 20–1
  and impact on team diversity,
    172
  and international experience,
    10–11
  and international literacy,
    10–11
  and managing paradoxes,
    16–17
  and national identity, 20–1
  and PM Theory of, 120–1
  and resilience, 14–15
  and self-evaluation: checklist,
    77; emotions, thinking
    and social behavior, 22
  and styles of, 172; cooperative,
    22–3; effects on
    performance, 121; "hero"
    model, 5; ideal, 30–1
  and succession management,
    11
  and team leadership, 22–3
  and team styles, 6
leadership courses, 18–19
Lee, Jill, 123, 166
  and Chinese leadership and
    teams, 124–6
Lee Kuan Yew, 117
Lewis, Richard, 104
Lonner, W., 150
Losada, M., 153

McAdam, John, 165–6
Mason, P. A., 38, 42, 132
mergers, 93
  and cultural change, 96
  and cultural differences, 92
  and culture shock, 93, 94, **95**
  and Executive Team Reviews,
    142–3

mergers – *continued*
  and failures of, 93–4
  and honeymoon phase, 94
  and impact on performance, 94
  and integration problems, 92–3
  and recovery phase, 94–5
  and shareholder value, 93–4, 95
  and uncertainty among employees, 94
metrics, and overreliance on, 90
Miles, R. E., 37–8, 131
Miller, Alex, 135
mindfulness, 119–20
Misumi, R., 120–1
Montaigne, Michel de, 19
Mooney, A. C., 174–5
multi-disciplinarity, and global teams, 66–7
M.video Ltd (Russia), 167, 168

national identity, and global leadership, 20–1
Netherlands, and non-national directors, 162
networking, and innovation, 155
nomination committees, and gender diversity, 170
Norway, and gender diversity, 168
Novogratz, Jacqueline, 40

Oberg, K., 53
obliquity, 58
observation, and innovation, 155
Olsen, B., 132
organizational structure, obsession with, 3–4

paradox, and dealing with, 16–17, 102
Parayitam, S., 132
Parott, W. G., 59
Pearson plc, 10
personal space, 105
Peterson, Randall, 22–3, 178
Petrofac plc, 163–4
Pettigrew, Andrew, 42, 43, 141, 182–3
philanthropic organizations, and global team development, 45–7
Pierce, Chris, 181–2
Pink, Daniel, 18, 154–5
Pitcher, P., 171–2
PM Leadership Theory, 120–1
Polman, Paul, 10
positive psychology, 152–3
post-traumatic stress disorder (PTSD), and cultural differences, 122–3
problem-solving
  and diverse teams, 54
  and emotions, 75, 119, 153
  and high performance teams, 25
  and homogenous teams, 6
  and team effectiveness, 33, 179
prospector organizations, 37–8
  and executive characteristics, 42
  and strengths of, 39
pseudo-teams, 33
psychological adaptation, 96–7
psychological androgyny, 17–20, 120
psychological assessment
  and cross-cultural assessments, 150–1

and cross-cultural differences in acceptability of, 147
as deficit oriented, 152
and Executive Team Reviews, 146–7
and factors affecting value of, 149–50
psychology–context–strategy model of team development, 51–2
and financial services case study, 73–4
and Top Team Health Check, 83–4
see also financial services, team development in

questioning, and innovation, 155

Ramaswamy, K., 42
rationality
  and assumptions of, 3, 15
  and business cultures, 59
recruitment, *see* search and selection processes; succession management
regulation, and growth of, 157
relationship-based approach to business, 57, 66, 67
remuneration, 105–6
resilience, 14–15, 53–4
  and building, 129
  and Chinese leaders, 122–3
  and components of, 154
  and emotions, 15, 53–4, 119, 154
  and individual resilience, 118–19
  and meaning of, 118
  and mindfulness, 119–20
  and social bonding, 103
  in teams, 120

risk
  and group decision-making, 182
  and management of, 14, 54, 181–2
Rockefeller Foundation, and global team development, 45–7
Rolls Royce, 133
Rosenfeld, H. M., 105
Rosen, Rich, 27

Sapienza, H. J., 174
Scardino, Marjorie, 10
Schein, E. H., 115, 116
Schoar, Antoinette, 136
Schwab, Klaus, 118
search and selection processes
  and best practices in CEO selection, 133–4
  and board members, 158
  and factors affecting candidate success, 44
  and failures in, 35–6
  and functional background of candidates, 37, 38
  and guidelines for, 37
  and importance of, 131
  and internal appointments, 133
  and need for improvement in, 35
  and need for values and strategy definition, 39–40
  and output experience of candidates, 38
  and questions to ask candidate, 40, 134, 136
  and search committee composition, 36

search and selection
processes – *continued*
and selecting on basis of
strategy, 36, 131
and selection criteria, 8–9,
47, 48–9
and strategic skills
assessment, 37–41
and throughput experience of
candidates, 38
and unconscious biases, 147–8
self, and Chinese view of, 122
shareholder value, and mergers,
93–4, 95
Singapore, 65
and China, 117
skills, and team development,
32, 34–44
and CEO selection: failures
in, 35; strategic skills
assessment, 37–41
and matching executive
characteristics and strategy,
42–4
Smith, A., 171–2
Smith, D. K., 32–4, 100, 101,
105, 106
Snow, C. C., 37–8, 131
social skills and behavior
and adaptive leadership, 20
and Culture Shock Triangle,
12
and impact of international
work, 62
and leadership, 60–2
and self-evaluation checklist,
22
socio-cultural adaptation,
96–7
Sonnenfeld, J., 174–5
South America, and business
culture, 59

Spain, and non-national
directors, 162
star performers, 17, 78
in auction business, 86–7
and management of, 83–4
stereotypical behavior, 75
strategy
and board's impact on, 182–3
and CEO selection, 36, 131;
strategic skills assessment,
37–41
and executive attributes, 38,
42
and lack of common
understanding of, 101–2
and match with executive
characteristics, 42–4
and organizational types, 37–8
and psychology–context–
strategy model of team
development, 51–2
and selection of board
members, 158
and succession management,
36
strengths-based assessment,
152–3
stress, 14–15
and management of, 118
and negative impact of, 75
and philanthropic
organizations, 46–7
and social support, 103
succession management, 133
in auction business, 88
and best practices in CEO
selection, 133–4
and Executive Team Reviews,
142
and factors affecting
candidate success, 44
and failures in, 35–6

and functional background, 37, 38
and global leadership, 11
and guidelines for, 37
and internal successors, 133
as key board responsibility, 44
and need for values and strategy definition, 39–40
and output experience of candidates, 38
and questions to ask candidate, 40, 134, 136
and search committee composition, 36
and selecting on basis of strategy, 36
and strategic skills assessment, 37–41
and throughput experience of candidates, 38
Sulzer AG (Switzerland), 166
Sussman, N. M., 105
Sutherland, Rory, 88–90, 106
  and advice for team leaders, 90
  and career of, 88–9
  and challenges in global teams, 89
  and creating effective culture, 89
  and creating the right behavior, 89
  and international client work, 89–90
  and providing purpose, 90
Sweden, and gender diversity, 168
Switzerland
  and gender diversity, 168
  and non-national directors, 162

Tappin, S., 16
Tata, 93
Tavistock Institute of Human Relations, 179, 181
team development, 44, 45–50
  and business challenges, 28
  and challenging the team, 102
  and coaching, 46
  and culture shock, 53
  and difficulties in quantifying impact of, 50
  and diversity management, 51, 64
  and dynamics, 32, 45–50
  and emerging markets, 63–5
  and establishing urgency and direction, 101
  and financial services, 47–50
  and first meetings, 101
  and goal-setting, 101
  and governance, 32–4, 112
  and key challenges in, 67
  and levels of, 31, 99
  and managing emotional side of, 53–4
  and managing thinking side of, 54–5
  and matching executive characteristics and strategy, 42–4
  and multi-disciplinarity, 66–7
  and observations on development initiatives, 29–30
  and performance improvement, 100
  and psychology–context–strategy model, 51–2
  and recruiting for future needs, 113
  and remuneration, 105–6

team development – *continued*
  and Rockefeller Foundation, 45–7
  and selection criteria, 47, 48–9
  and skills, 32, 34–44
  and spending time together, 102–3
  and strategic skills assessment, 37–41
  and success factors in, 71–3
  and systemic change, **99**
  and team retreats, 46
  and Top Team Health Check, **83–4**
  and trust, 113
  and vagueness of term, 29
  see also dynamics; financial services; governance; skills; turnaround case study
team retreats, and team development, 46
teams
  and challenges in managing, 175–6
  and challenges in managing global, 87
  and complementarity, 6
  and definition of, 33, 100
  and definition of high-performance teams, 34
  and distinction from working groups, 33, 34
  and ideal number of members, 1
  and main challenge faced by, 69
  and need for diversity, 7
  and perceptions of effectiveness of, 1, 27
  and pseudo-teams, 33
  and success undermined by qualities required for success, 68
  and team types, 6–7
technology sector, and team development, 68–9
Tesco, 133
thinking
  and Culture Shock Triangle, **12**
  and managing culture shock, 54–5
  and psychological androgyny, 17–20
  and self-evaluation checklist, 22
Thomas, A. S., 42
360° feedback, and Executive Team Reviews, 151–2
top management teams (TMTs), 5–6, 37
  and conflict management, 173–5
  and impact of characteristics on company performance, 132
  and impact of diversity, 171
  and impact of leadership styles, 172
  and perceptions of team effectiveness, 27
  and priority of talent over structure, 140
  and state of governance in, 101–3
Top Team Health Check, **83–4**
transaction-based approach to business, 66, 67
transnational community of business leaders, 59, 60
  and global nomads, 20–1
  and identity, 62

Trompenaars, F., 55–6, 57
trust, and development of, 113
Tugdale, M. M., 118
turnaround case study, and cultural change, 97–8, 106–7
 and approach to, 98–100
 and governance workshops, 110–11
 and impact of team development intervention, 112
 and individual development, 108–9
 and initial team weaknesses, 107
 and starting from the top, 107
 and team culture, 111–12
 and team development agenda, **110**
 and team development goals, 108
 and team governance, 111
 and team profile, 109, **110**
 see also Virgin Media
Twigg, N., 132
Type A executives, 57, 75, 78, 147

Unilever, 10
United Kingdom
 and average tenure of CEOs, 131
 and business culture, 58–9, 116, **117**
 and diversity of boards, 159, **160**; characteristics of women board members, 169; decline in, 159
 and foreign-born CEOs, 60, 161
 and international experience of CEOs, 10, 59–60
 and non-national directors, 162
 and succession management, 133
United States
 and emotional expression, 59, 104–5
 and gender diversity on boards, 168
 and limited international experience of CEOs, 10
 and non-national directors, 162
 and succession management, 133
 and work/life overlap, 103–4
Upper Echelon Theory, 37, 38, 132

Virgin Media, and turnaround of
 aligning leaders to purpose, 127–8
 attracting great leaders, 126–7
 creating great leaders, 128–9

Walker, David, 26, 179
Walker Review (2009), 179–81
Welch, Jack, 61, 133
Williams, Mark, 119–20
working groups, and distinction from teams, 33, **34**
work/life overlap, and cultural differences, 103–4
World Economic Forum (Davos, 2013), 118, 119

Yun Jong-Yong, 135

Zehnder, Egon, 162, 168
Zimmerman, M. A., 173

The manufacturer's authorised representative in the EU is Springer Nature Customer Service Centre GmbH, Europaplatz 3, 69115 Heidelberg, Germany. If you have any concerns regarding our products, please contact ProductSafety@springernature.com

Printed and bound by CPI Group (UK) Ltd, Croydon, CR0 4YY

26/03/2026

02078976-0001